BILLY CONNOLLY'S
TRACKS ACROSS
AMERICA

SPHERE

First published in Great Britain in 2016 by Sphere

Photography by Jaimie Gramston with additional stills by Mike Reilly.

Design and illustrations by D.R. ink

Endpapers – Creative Jen Designs/Shutterstock; page 203 – Jazle/iStock;
page 280–281 – aarrows/Shutterstock

1 3 5 7 9 10 8 6 4 2

A CIP catalogue record for this book
is available from the British Library.

ISBN 978-0-7515-6413-6

Printed in Italy

Papers used by Sphere are from well-managed forests
and other responsible sources.

MIX
Paper from
responsible sources
FSC® C104740

Sphere
An imprint of
Little, Brown Book Group
Carmelite House
50 Victoria Embankment
London EC4Y 0DZ

An Hachette UK Company
www.hachette.co.uk

www.littlebrown.co.uk

BILLY CONNOLLY'S
TRACKS ACROSS
AMERICA

with Matt Whyman

sphere

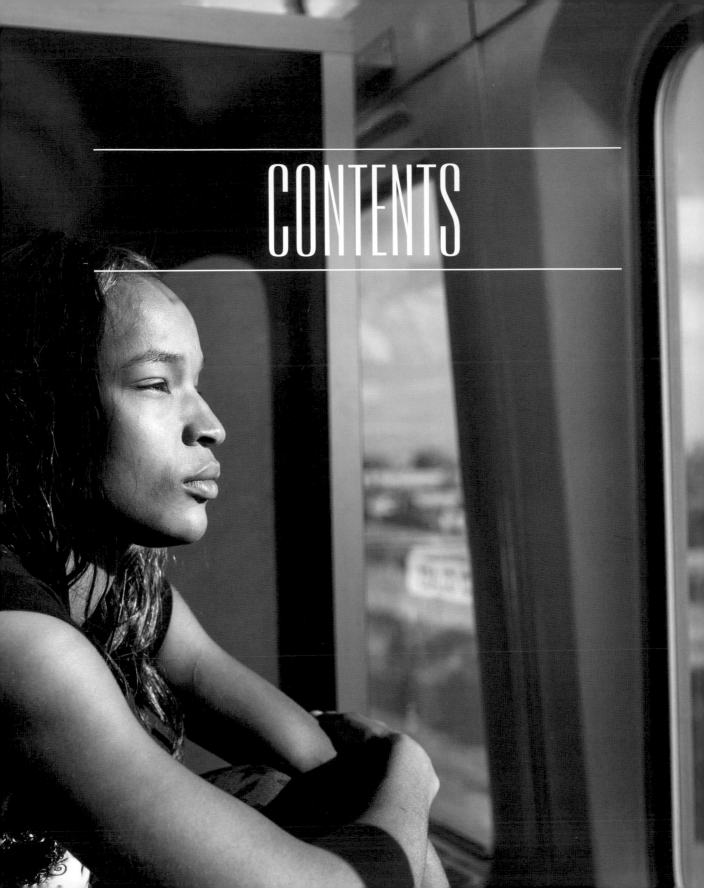

CONTENTS

INTRODUCTION 6–9

CHICAGO TO SEATTLE

SEATTLE TO EL PASO

EL PASO TO NEW YORK

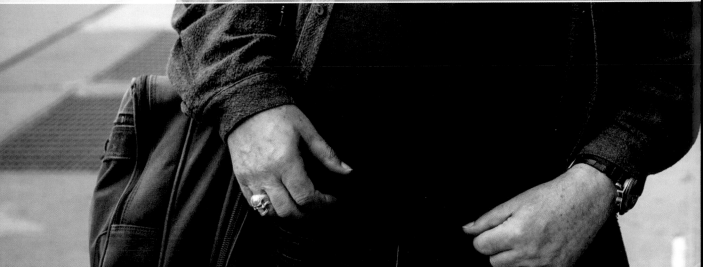

INTRODUCTION

Hail fine fellows – it is I, Billy, back once again to invite you on a magical adventure.

I've lived in America almost half of my life now. In that time, I've seen a lot of airports and quite a few cities, but not much in between.

But that, my friends, is about to change because I'm taking the train into the back yard of America. We're heading to the places you never get to see thirty thousand feet in the air. And my route – Chicago to New York, the wrong way round – is the story of this nation. Eight thousand miles and fifteen states steeped in living history. We'll be joining trains with names rich in promise – the *Empire Builder*, the *Sunset Limited*, the *Coast Starlight* and the *Crescent* – riding the tracks that took cowboys to their ranches, drifters to the sea, as well as immigrants, fortune chasers and escapees to all points of the compass. Moving through some of the most spectacular vistas you'll ever see, it's a great big, fat, epic story about people.

A nice little day trip, eh? So why not come with me? We're sure to have a load of fun.

I'm in good company for this journey, too. It isn't my film crew, though they are lovely. Nor do I have my fellow train travellers in mind, who are equally fragrant. No, I'm talking about the spirit orphans … *Ach, Billy's finally lost it*, I hear you say, but bear with me while I tell you a wee story, because I think it'll persuade you to come on board for the ride.

The tale plays out in an old, unassuming song by a folk singer called Utah Phillips. Born in 1935, Utah was a mighty, humble and very playful man. I'm sure he'd be very proud of the fact that he's often described as a dishwasher and labour activist. Utah was also a committed train hopper. He loved to ride the boxcars and sing about the plight of ordinary people, and I recommend you check out his body of work because it really touches the soul, you know? But the song I have in mind, 'Orphan Train', shines a light on a time when kids without homes were packed on trains and sent across the country. The train would stop at stations along the way. Each time, these girls and boys would be made to get out and line up on parade. Then, farmers and suchlike would come down and pick off a child and take them in. Those poor wee buggers! Can you imagine that happening today? Their plight certainly had an impact on Utah Phillips, and the song he wrote about them is truly haunting. The orphan trains reached the end of the line in the early Fifties, but it's fresh in my mind as I prepare for the journey ahead. And I hope they'll be with us in spirit along the way.

ONE

CHICAGO TO SEATTLE

We're westward bound for the first leg of our journey. Rich in anecdote and history, our two-thousand-mile trek follows the great migration by the first European settlers. On a personal level, this is the America of my cinema childhood. From the window of my carriage, I'll be looking out at vistas straight off the silver screen and daydreaming about the pioneers that crossed this once uncharted landscape.

My bonnie steed for our first leg of the trip is the *Empire Builder*. It's a passenger train operated by Amtrak across the mid-western and north-western states. The company's busiest long-distance line, it's been running since the 1920s. Every year, this hard-working and undeniably handsome silver devil carries over half a million people across the country, and will transport us all the way from Chicago to Seattle. We'll explore the vast plains of Minnesota and North Dakota, the big sky country of Montana, then on to Washington State. It's a ride that will take us through places we've heard of but rarely see and we'll meet the characters that define them.

So, hop aboard with me. There are cups of tea to be enjoyed, sights to behold and loafing to be had.

Chicago Union Station ①

Minnesota ②

North Dakota ①

Montana

4

Seattle

5

CHICAGO UNION STATION

Welcome to Chicago! It's the most windswept and interesting city in America. But I'm not here to hang around. This is where my journey begins…

THE GRAND DEPARTURE

As soon as I set foot inside the station's Great Hall, my sneakers make a lovely squeaky noise. It's like being in the gym at school all over again and brings a grin to my face. The place is also vast. It's like a marble cathedral – a temple to transport fronted by Corinthian columns, bathed in soft lighting and crowned with a vaulted glass roof. Public announcements fill the air, almost inaudible in this echo chamber, but a sound that tells me that I'm set to go places. Above all, it reminds me of going on family holidays as a little boy back in Scotland.

This isn't the first station to be built here, just to the west of the river between West Jackson Boulevard and West Adams Street. I can only think the city planners weren't satisfied until they had a railway terminal that could easily double as a palace. Looking up and around, I spot two grand statues in the upper reaches, high above the throng of travellers. One figure is supporting an owl on its arm and another holds a cockerel. These guys represent night and day and embody the fact that we're in a space that never closes its doors. Chicago Union Station runs right around the clock, dispatching passengers and welcoming weary travellers from afar.

The men's lounge is a surprise to find in this day and age, and a delight. Old-timers sit back in comfy chairs with their knees spread wide and broadsheet newspapers in their hands. A younger generation of guys also use this space, perched on high stools browsing laptops. But once upon a time this was more than just a waiting room for the ugly sex. The oasis of calm and concentration is host to framed photographs from a bygone age, but it's the nicotine-stained wall tiles that bring it vividly alive. They're supposed to be a nice cream colour and yet the shades of yellow and brown paint a picture of a time I find compelling.

The barber's shop was once a popular hang-out for gentlemen ahead of their long journeys. One of the first photos I see captures a big fat guy in the barber's chair awaiting his short back and sides. He's wearing a bib around his neck and has a stogie plugged in his mouth and another two in his top pocket – ready to go. I don't know, though. Maybe he's hiding a machine

gun under there, too. He'll certainly be getting himself a shoeshine at the same time and leave feeling like a million dollars. That world has gone now, but I like the idea very much. It's a beautiful room and well worth a few minutes of any traveller's time.

For a nation that prides itself on looking forward, there's something curiously old-fashioned about the American rail system. Making my way to the platform, I pass porters pushing luggage trolleys and a conductor checking his fob watch. Make no mistake – getting the train here is an *event*.

The *Empire Builder*, as train names go, sounds a bit more exciting than 'the 5.40 to Didcot'. And that's as it should be, as we prepare to sweep across a landscape steeped in history. Someone once said that businessmen fly and dreamers catch trains, and this is a route that thousands – if not millions – of dreamers have taken. Fashions and hairstyles may change, of course, but the dreams are just the same: a new life, an old flame or just the draw of a great escape. I only have to look around to see that this is about to become a train full of dreamers. There are passengers from every generation here, from couples to friends, families, loners and lonely-hearts. Every one of them has a story to tell and I'm glad to be in their company. It's exciting to hear the last carriage doors slam shut and the stationmaster's whistle blow.

'So long, Chicago, so-o-o long … *Yeah!*' he announces like a jazz compère and a moment later we ease off on our way.

On board, I find a good place to settle in and stow my luggage overhead. Strikingly, this train offers some seats facing the window. If you're the kind of passenger who prefers to tune out and watch the world pass by, this is the railroad for you. Me? I'm happy to take a table seat in true British fashion. As well as admiring the ever-changing landscape, and picking at my banjo, I like to doze as well as chat to anyone who cares to share my table. Having a camera crew with me is certainly a great ice-breaker. When I venture along the aisle to seek out the restaurant carriage, and find out what draws people to this choice of travel, I feel like I should have a Mariachi band right behind me.

'This is the only way to go,' drawls one old boy at his table and salutes me with his drink. 'You have the freedom to walk around,' he adds, clearly enjoying this prime time of his life, 'and maybe enjoy a margarita.'

Even in our first few miles out of Chicago, there's an atmosphere of camaraderie on board. Two girls giggle and hoot about how nervous they'd be had they hit the road, sharing the lanes with eighteen-wheel trucks and the threat of a breakdown or puncture. The crew tells me about a silver-haired couple they've met, who happily bickered about whether their lifelong romance began with love at first sight. He was adamant that she was the one from the moment he set eyes on her, but she begged to differ.

I'm told he shot her a look. She chuckled and tickled him in the ribs, as besotted now as she was back then.

'It was love at *second* sight,' she insisted with a twinkle in her eye. 'We first met on a train, and I never even thought about it then.'

The train is a great place to ponder and reflect, I think. At my time of life I reminisce a lot and it reminds me of the role trains played in my childhood. As a family, we would go on holiday to the Clyde. To get there, we'd take a train from Glasgow Central Station to Winsway. Even now, I remember how the engine driver would be hanging out of the front wearing one of those hats that were shiny on top. And he would always say, 'Hello kid, how are you doing?' and you could see the glow of the firebox and all that. There was a romance to it, you know?

Now, I'm not exactly a train nut. I like them, but I'm not the kind of guy who ever dreamed of being an engine driver. As a child, of course, I used to have a train set. I never got one of those fancy electric ones. Mine was the clockwork variety. On the box there was a picture of a huge locomotive blazing through the night. On the footplate stood hard-working men caked in soot. In my excitement, I'd open the box to find just this wee engine with three carriages and a few lengths of track that formed a circle, at best. Inevitably, I quickly got bored of it. To liven things up I'd muster my toy soldiers and lay them down across the track. Once that peril was over, my next trick would be to leave a bit of the track missing so the engine would career across the floor. Warm memories, you know, but nothing that fired up an ambition to drive one for real. As a passenger on the *Empire Builder*, though, I'm sold. Sitting at the window, watching the world whisk by, I'm as happy looking forward as I am thinking back through the years.

My first night on board was pleasant enough, even though it took some getting used to. I settled down in my wee bunk, but it struck me as being kind of noisy.

My only other experience of a train sleeper was in Britain and that didn't go well. I was shaken from head to foot, squashed into a cramped and sweaty bunk and I failed to get a wink of sleep. This time, it was the train's whistle that made me wonder if I would ever nod off. Every few minutes or so, just as my eyelids grew heavy I'd hear a *HOOO-HOOO* and that was it. I thought that whistle was to scare animals off the track or something, but apparently they're legally bound to do it every time they approach a crossing. So, there must be a lot of crossings on this line and after a time I began to enjoy it. Then there's the constant movement. In the UK, it felt like I was being wrestled from my bunk by an unseen force, but this was different. It was more a case of being gently rocked from side to side – in a way it's like being in your mother's arms. Together with the whistle, which began to sound quite reassuring as we travelled through the night, it became a rather jolly experience.

I can't say the same for my morning shower, unfortunately. I nearly broke my bloody neck as we trundled along. As you probably know I've got Parkinson's disease. In my experience, people with Parkinson's should not have showers on trains in much the same way that Vietnam veterans shouldn't go to firework displays in swamps. That's a bad state to be in. But despite the ordeal I survived feeling refreshed and by the time we approach our first stop along the way I'm frankly quite excited. As we pull in, the guard reminds us to take everything with us, including children, he jokes, because they can be a little hard to return. I don't have any kids with me, but I feel like one as I hop off onto the platform with high hopes for a memorable day ahead.

MINNESOTA

This is a state with a lot of lakes. Under a bright sun on a clear day, what better way to behold such sparkly splendour than by train?

We're heading for St Paul, a metropolitan area alongside Minneapolis, and a nice, quiet place it appears to be. Once upon time, however, this Minnesotan capital was home to legendary baddies and bank robbers like 'Baby Face' Nelson, 'Machine Gun' Kelly and Ma Barker, as well as a guy called Alvin 'Creepy' Karpis, which is the best name I've heard in years. It was Creepy Karpis who said that St Paul was heaven for gangsters. He reckoned that if you had two friends and you hadn't seen them in a while, they were either in jail or in St Paul, which is weird because Norwegian Lutherans were the first to settle here and lay the foundations for the town. These were peaceful, pastoral folk. Hardly gangsters, d'you know what I mean? Anyway, I'm excited by my visit here, because every year the town is host to a rather wonderful and typically American celebration of the great outdoors.

MINNESOTA STATE FAIR: A STATE OF WONDER

For twelve days every year, people from all corners of the region gather on these grounds to be charmed, well fed, enlightened and entertained in equal measure. The Minnesota State Fair goes way beyond just looking at livestock. There are competitions to enter, processions to applaud, music to appreciate and … sculptures to behold made from butter. Yes, butter. The first thing to note is that the State Fair is a very big deal indeed. This is one of the largest in the USA, but despite the throngs and the cost involved, my first impression is of a lovely sense of innocence. It's a bright and breezy day. Families drift from one attraction to the next, the kids clutching candy floss on a stick or a balloon that's bound to slip their grip and float away before the day is done.

The fair started as an agricultural show in 1859, the year after Minnesota became a state. Since then, it's only ever been cancelled on four occasions. In 1861, shortly after the annual event had begun, civil war broke out. One year later, the Dakota Indian Uprising kept the gates closed. In 1945, World War Two cast a shadow over proceedings, while twelve months later a polio epidemic persuaded the organisers that mingling crowds might not be such a smart idea. All in all, it beats cancelling a major event due to bad weather.

There isn't much that stops these guys from celebrating their way of life.

The good news is that no major catastrophe has put a stop to the fun and games for me now. Walking through the gates, I'm spoiled for choice by so many attractions. Despite the pomp and spectacle of the college marching band, which America does exceptionally well, I can't take my eyes off a sign that promises so much: The Miracle of Birth. I wonder what I might find inside the big tent. Will it be like the opposite of a bullfight, with a happy outcome for the animals involved? I sincerely hope so.

As it turns out, the Miracle of Birth does what it says on the tin. In a pen surrounded by awestruck onlookers, a new-born calf sits in the straw on buckled legs, just minutes into the world. Another pen contains a great big fat pig on her side with a tiny litter attached to her teats, but it's the calf that has seized my attention. This is the one I want to see. Mother Cow licks and nudges the wee thing, encouraging him to grasp this opportunity for life. As I find a gap to get a good view, the woman providing the commentary mentions something about the 'vaginal canal' and I know this must be serious stuff. Neither mother nor offspring seems remotely concerned that this magical bonding moment is happening in front of an audience. If anything, I like to think the encouraging noises we're all making finally persuade the calf to have a bash at standing. He does so unsteadily, but that's quite enough for me to join in with everyone else and mark the moment with a heartfelt cheer. It's a wonderful moment, made all the more special because so many children witness it. There's something raw and really healthy about this, I think. A true education. It has made my day and there's still so much to see.

As a Scot, I can't resist the sight of Highland cattle. With their long horns and wavy – almost feminine – coats, they're unmistakable as a breed. The moment I lay eyes on a pair, grazing serenely in their display pen, I make my way straight over and engage the proud owner in conversation.

'This one is called Grit,' he says proudly, 'and the other one is Tegan.'

I nod, unconvinced, and tell him they should all be called Hamish. He laughs, both thumbs tucked into his belt loop, and tries out the name for size.

'My daughters once owned some,' I tell him. 'They're big beasties, but I couldn't believe how timid they could be.'

'That's right,' he says, nodding. 'Were they all called Hamish?'

I tell him they overruled me on that occasion and named them after hairdressers.

'We had Tony,' I say, 'and Guy.'

Inevitably, given that we're standing before cattle with longer tresses than mine, our conversation moves on to the styling possibilities.

'We have youngsters who work on the farm,' he says, and then appears to weigh the air with both hands. 'They like to give them hairdos.'

'Really?'

'Oh, sure. Especially before a show like this one,' he adds, and turns again to admire his livestock. 'They've both been shampooed this morning.'

I can't resist reaching out to have a touch.

'Soft,' I say, running my fingers through their lustrous locks.

'Spunky,' he adds.

'Right,' I say, and take a step back.

It reminds me of the cow we once kept who sported a lovely blonde forelock. So we called her Veronica, after Veronica Lake the great film actress, who was fondly known as 'the girl with the peekaboo hair'.

My new friend knows just what I mean and agrees when I say that in a funny way it's a shame that people have taken the breed to their hearts, because from a farming point of view the meat is exceptional. In Scotland, I tell him, some people with land like to have Highland cattle as living ornaments because they look so striking.

'Same in the States,' he says, which just goes to show that a handsome cow can charm the world over.

It also reminds me why I'm so fond of this breed.

'At milking time back home,' I say, 'the farmers put wellies over their horns to avoid being accidentally stabbed.'

'Uh huh.'

My man here looks me in the eye as if uncertain whether to believe me. I am being absolutely serious, however.

'I thought it was an international thing,' I tell him. 'Nobody wants to risk being stabbed in the arse when a cow turns around to see what's going on, right?'

'I guess.' He rubs his chin, thinking things through.

I have an urge to tell him that the middle-class cows go for green wellies and the working class stick with black, but I don't think he'll buy it. Instead, we part company having bonded over a breed of cattle that can never be beaten for Best Hair in Show.

Leaving the tents behind, I'm delighted to find a procession in full swing now. It's a marvellous affair and all the bands are well presented and beautifully choreographed. Not so the Vietnam War vets. There's just two guys holding a banner aloft and I wonder why there's nobody marching behind. Maybe they're watching the Miracle of Birth, I think to myself. The American Legion is also thinly represented, but I like how the clutch of soldiers in their number pass by as if anticipating an ambush. Vintage jeeps and vehicles from World War Two follow close behind. I half expect to see Bob Hope swing by, waving from the turret of a tank. Then come the flatbed trucks transformed into festive floats. They carry men and women in all kinds of costume, depending on the cause they're supporting. I wave at a dejected-looking lion, who picks up considerably and waves back at me. Undeniably, Princess Kay of the Milky Way gives me a nod and a wink that suggest my luck might be in, and I'm delighted to see the giant model of an Aberdeen Angus on wheels. Finally, a string of little kids riding plastic farm animals on wheels trundle by, towed by a little tractor. It really is a celebration of the people, from war heroes to proud farming folk and bemused wee children wondering why the man with the silver hair and oval shades is chuckling as they pass.

I'm still smiling to myself when I inspect the scarecrow competition. Whoever decided that these things needed judging was both insane and inspired, and I love them for it. The entrants range from hugely inventive to sweetly whimsical. I check out the Lady and the Tramp, presumably one for each end of the field, the well-dressed bunny in a boater and the Donald Trump lookalike, which must surely do a good job keeping the birds from the crops.

One even has a poem pinned to its pocket that reads:

Mornings are bright
My hair looks a fright
The coffee was hot
I drank the whole pot
It's a wonderful day
To scare crows away.

In my view, the most original scarecrow in this year's competition is the giant crow. It's larger than life, with a broom handle for a spine and wings that droop low to the ground. I have no doubt the birds take one look at this diabolical apparition and take wing at once. Every one of these exhibits is a winner and I hope they get the credit they deserve. The same goes for the table displaying this year's crop of corn seed creations. This is another American tradition that involves creating fine images – and sometimes objects – using corn seeds, ears, husks and stalks. I'm taken with the recreation of Trump's magnificent hair – the man appears to be a running theme here – as well as the portrait of a protest with banners that read 'Black Lives Matter', and the cowboy boots look good enough to slip on. I'm not sure I'd get very far in them, mind. In some ways this comes very close to macaroni art. So much of it is really clever, from the playful to the political, and a display of utter devotion to the craft. Even if the finished pieces aren't the kind of thing you'd display on your mantelpiece back home, you have to admire the dedication and creativity.

So, what could possibly follow a corn art display? A corn competition, of course! I wish it aimed to crown the most Cornish corn of the season, but sadly these folk take it far more seriously. I haven't the foggiest what distinguishes one ear of corn from another. Even when I find the entrant with the winner's rosette, I have to admit to being stumped. It looks identical to all the others. Even so, I can imagine that somewhere out there in Minnesota a farmer headed back home from the fields, produced a bunch of corn for his wife to admire, and said, 'Will you look at that?', and she only had to glance at it to reply, 'That's a prize-winner if ever I saw one. We should enter it for the State Fair.' I like to think that's what's happened, at any rate.

Having had my fill of corn for one day, or even the whole year, I think I'm now stumbling upon a religious cult: a crowd of youngsters dressed in shades of earthy brown, like cheerleaders of the soil, are crammed onto the stairs behind a glass door. For some reason they're singing their hearts out in unison. A security guy has also noticed them and eggs them on to sing louder. Finally, someone opens the door and they spill out with wide smiles and in a state of high excitement.

There's only one thing for it, I decide. I must follow them and find out where they're heading.

A few minutes later, the troupe is up on stage, dancing, singing and fist-pumping with unbridled zeal to a huge audience. Now I love a school play like any other parent. I also reserve the right to make a quiet exit when they break into 'The Final Countdown'.

Back outside, I find the animal impersonation competition in progress. Naturally, I approach with a great sense of glee. We've all had a bash at making farmyard noises at some time in our lives, right? From the cluck of the hen to the moo of a cow, there's not a soul on this planet who hasn't checked that nobody is within earshot and then given it their best shot. Of course, there are some who are brave enough to impersonate animals in public, so why not hold an event to find the most convincing?

I join the throng midway through the competition. A sparky young girl has taken the microphone and is preparing the audience for what they are about to hear.

'I'll be doing a horse,' she tells them, before inhaling sharply and then blowing as hard as she can through slackened lips while shaking her head to and fro.

It's brilliant. I am completely bemused and it deserves the huge round of applause it receives.

Next up, a direct challenge to Horse Girl. The confident young lady who steps forward is wearing a sash from winning some earlier competition. She warns the crowd that they might not see this one coming and I hold my breath, along with everyone else.

'Mooooo,' she intones into the microphone, and with that her turn in the spotlight is over.

The next in line, Fanny, bounds on with her arms aloft like she's the winner in waiting. Clearly pleased to see her, the compère asks if that was an interpretative dance ahead of her performance. Fanny answers no, seemingly assured by what she's about to offer, and then commands silence from her audience.

To be fair, Fanny's angry cockerel impression is pretty decent. Way better than the next guy's falsetto cow. Between ourselves, I've never heard cattle hit the high notes before – maybe they breed them differently in these parts. From there on out, the competition becomes stiffer still, with the appearance of a turkey and a deeply convincing goat. I didn't expect to hear a bison, but I guess they're a popular feature of the landscape. Had you told me that they make a noise like someone being sick into a gutter on a Friday night, I might've questioned if you'd been drinking yourself. Given the wild reception the impersonator receives, I guess they really do sound like they're barfing. I can't tell you who claimed the crown as best animal impersonator because I had a train to catch, but I can confirm that everyone was a winner in my eyes.

When I left the Minnesota State Fair, I realised I had been smiling for most of the day. It's a lovely feeling, and much of this is down to the air of innocence pervading the event. It may have been staged on a grand scale, but it still had the feeling of a country fête. Anyone could get involved – d'you know what I mean? Half of the animal impersonators were terrible, but had they been professional it would've been a soulless affair. To my ear, the shabby bleat of a sheep beats a well-rehearsed cluck any day, because it's all about finding the courage and self-deprecation to stand up and give it a shot. Mercifully, I wasn't asked to join in, but I did try out a tired moo when the film crew weren't listening. It was pretty good actually, even if I do say so myself. Maybe I should've found the guts to try it out in public. Now I'll never know if I stood a chance of winning the top prize.

THE JUICY LUCY BURGER: HAMBURGER HEAVEN

Minneapolis is only a short ride from St Paul. It may have been made famous by Prince and Paisley Park, with other notable names associated with the city including Billy Graham the evangelist, Bob Dylan and the novelist Anne Tyler, but it's also the home of another product that deserves worldwide attention: the Juicy Lucy Burger. It's earned this name for a reason. The 'juice' part is down to the cheese. It's molten hot and not just layered on top of the patty like some dairy duvet. It's embedded snugly within the beef itself. A lagoon of cheese, if you like. Apparently, you have to be careful when you take a bite in case it squishes out and takes the skin off the inside of your mouth.

In 2014, the city's finest burger received the ultimate accolade when the President of the United States of America paid a visit to see what all the fuss was about. If it's good enough to draw Barack Obama, I think to myself, as I approach the eatery that claims responsibility for the creation, then it must be something special.

Matt's Bar is an unassuming building on a corner between two blocks. It first opened in the 1950s. When our man Matt first purchased the place, the burger wasn't on the menu. It was a customer who first gave him the idea. Like a true barstool philosopher, he suggested putting cheese inside two meat patties and sealing it up. So Matt gave it a shot. He put the burger together, served it up and invited the guy to try it. As soon as he took a bite, he hit the pool of cheese and it splurged right out. According to local folklore, this chappie thought it was just terrific. He stood up and declared: 'Now, that's a Juicy Lucy!', and in the same breath burger history was made.

Inside the bar I meet Paul, the current manager and champion of Matt's invention. A super-friendly middle-aged guy with an impressive head of ginger dreadlocks and both arms solid with tattoos, Paul is only too happy to recount the day the leader of the First World dropped in and ordered lunch. We sit facing one another at a table where I've just been served a Juicy Lucy, of course.

'It was a bit of a surprise,' he says, and chuckles at his understatement. 'We only found out he was coming about thirty-five minutes before. Basically, this gentleman came in, pulled me aside, and told me to prepare for the President.'

I picture Matt's Bar overrun with Men in Black, which turns out not to be too far from the truth.

'Within half an hour the Secret Service were everywhere,' he continues, 'and then without warning Mr Obama walked in through the front door.'

'That's brilliant,' I say, taking my first tentative mouthful of the bar's famous burger. It tastes delicious, but I'm nervous about biting into the cheese locked inside and melting my molars away. 'Did you have any customers at the time?'

'Oh, it was as busy as this,' he says, and gestures at the tables and the bar. It's pretty much full, I realise, and it must've been a treat for everyone to see the President step up to make his order. Paul adopts a bittersweet expression when I share this and tells me that earlier that same day the bar's founder, Matt, had passed away at almost ninety years of age.

'Oh,' I say, a little taken aback at such timing. 'I'm sorry to hear that.'

'Actually, we see it as a fitting tribute to him,' Paul offers, and he's right. 'To serve the US President was a testimony to everything Matt had built.'

Leaving Paul to his thoughts for a second, I venture a little further into my burger. It certainly feels hotter the further I go and I'm still wary, as if I'm on some journey to the centre of the earth. When I look across the table again I find that, like a proud father, Paul is back watching me munch away.

'I like your ink,' I say with my mouth full, just to distract him while I mop ketchup from my chin.

Paul considers his arms like he's never noticed the tattoos before.

'Thanks,' he says. 'It started with one and then went from there.'

'You don't have a Juicy Lucy on there do you?' I ask, not seriously because I can't imagine anyone being tempted to ink a burger onto their skin.

Paul shows me a space under his left elbow and I stand pleasantly corrected.

'I had to do it,' he grins as I admire the artwork.

While he goes on to delve deeper into the history of the bar, I brave going for the heart of the burger. It's cooled sufficiently so I don't incinerate my mouth – the cheese is lovely and gooey, just pleasantly coating the inside of my mouth. Straight away, I realise why Matt's bar has been serving customers for six decades.

'It really does taste incredible,' I say. 'Have you always been in the burger business?'

Paul considers my question with a smile that tells me he's a little embarrassed.

'I'm from the financial world originally,' he confesses after a moment, and I struggle not to splutter my food across the table. 'Investments.'

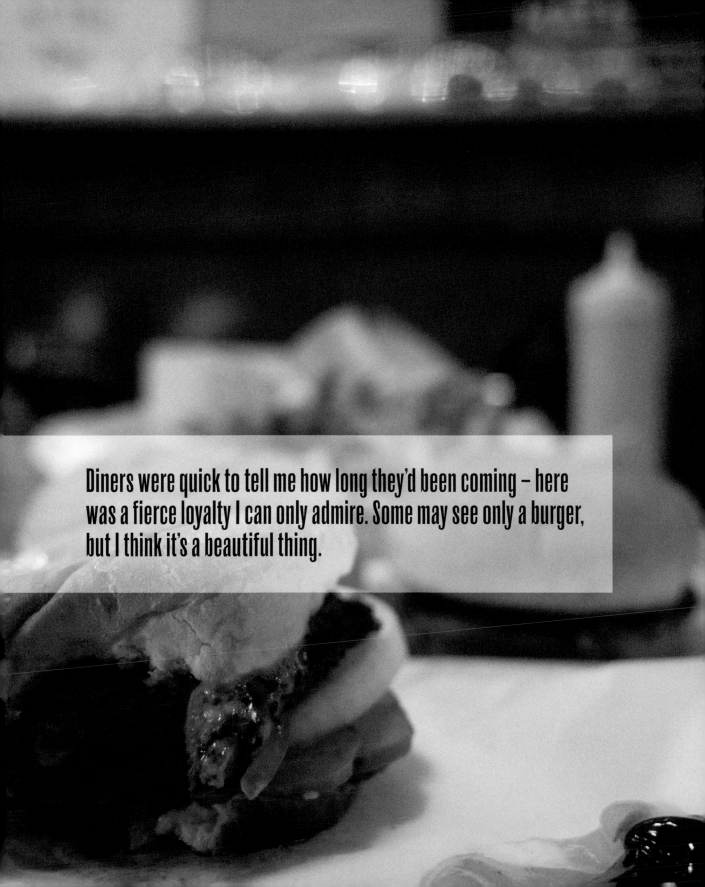

Diners were quick to tell me how long they'd been coming – here was a fierce loyalty I can only admire. Some may see only a burger, but I think it's a beautiful thing.

As I learn why someone would choose to make the switch from stocks and shares to serving customers in a saloon – and who wouldn't? – I relish the last of my burger. Later, back on the train, I realise the memory of that Juicy Lucy will remain with me for the rest of my life. I love the way Americans will take something so simple and then fawn over it as if it was a new-born baby. These guys didn't feel the need to make it the size of a manhole cover, as you might expect in the States, or to go overboard with the gimmicks by putting another cheese inside the cheese or some such and calling it a SuperDuper Juicy Lucy, Matt's Bar simply offers a chance for people to appreciate a good thing very well done. You could have two, if you fancied it, and not feel ill in the street afterwards from stuffing yourself silly. After Paul returned to the bar, the diners at nearby tables were quick to tell me how long they'd been coming. For up to fifteen years, it emerged – here was a fierce loyalty I can only admire. Some may see only a burger, but I think it's a beautiful thing.

THE MALL WALKERS OF MINNEAPOLIS: KEEP ON MOVIN'!

The USA doesn't do shopping like we do, and I've heard about a mall that hammers home the difference. This is no shabby parade on a wet Tuesday afternoon, and even if it's raining that won't be a problem. Here, you don't just pop out for half an hour to pick up the bread and the tea bags. Oh, no. People come for the best part of a day, and not just to browse and buy. For some, it's a lifestyle choice that keeps them fit and healthy – and even prolongs their lives. Now as soon as I heard this claim, I felt it needed some investigating. So some of the crew went to the city's largest temple of commerce, the Mall of America, where they met a lively band of seniors who sounded like a squad of veteran renegades from *Star Wars* … The mall walkers. This is the story they brought back to the train for me:

'What brought me was the knee surgery,' said one bespectacled lady, once the crew had tracked them down on an upper floor of this gigantic shrine to shopping. There were some half-dozen in total, in the autumn or the winter of their years, and all made the crew feel quite welcome when they accompanied them for a wee while. Some negotiate the marble floor unaided and glide along in their full-length dresses as if drawn by an invisible winch. A few rely on sticks and zimmer frames to keep them upright. What unites them all, however is their determination to stay mobile when others would settle for a snooze in a sunny spot. But why choose to stretch your legs in a shopping mall? What's wrong with the great outdoors? 'It's bumpy,' the lady with the glasses had said, as if she tried it once and learned a painful lesson. 'You can trip over things.'

'And, hey, this is Minnesota!' the lady beside her chipped in, dressed impeccably in cream to match her hair; and she began to chuckle. 'This state has very hard winters. You don't walk outside in those conditions.'

'In here, it's warm and the floor is smooth,' their first pal continued, and gestured at the stores as they slowly passed by. 'Heck, we're in a safe and beautiful space, right?'

The mall walkers advance at a pace that wouldn't challenge a snail. But even though the mall is huge, and the walkers wouldn't be able to cover a floor until Christmas next year at the pace they walk at, time spent with them sounds like a pleasure. Their marathon-running days might be long gone, but why not stay active in a way that keeps them happy and out of harm's way? I hate shopping at the best of times but the sight of a platinum-haired party crawling along at their leisure would bring a smile to my face, and God bless them for that.

Over the course of half an hour, other groups were spotted across the galleries, all moving at a similar pace, as if a speed restriction might be in place.

I learn from the crew that the leader is ninety-seven years of age and still going strong, and as I hear more about them I begin to appreciate the essence of what draws these guys together. It isn't just fitness, but friendship too. There's a great camaraderie that binds this group. It's clear that everyone knows each other's business and are stronger for it. Just before the team leaves, the lady in cream reports what brought her to the group.

'Ten years ago I was in a car with my husband when he died behind the wheel,' she told them, with the controlled composure of someone who has retold this terrible tragedy many times before. 'It happened during an ice storm, and

Here, you don't just pop out for half an hour to pick up the bread and the tea bags. Oh, no. People come for the best part of a day, and not just to browse and buy. For some, it's a lifestyle choice that keeps them fit and healthy – and even prolongs their lives.

somehow I had to stop the car. We travelled at least half a mile before we came to a standstill. The experience was such a shock that I suffered heart failure.

'You know, I actually think my heart had broken,' she continued, her voice tightening by a jot. 'The months that followed were awful, but it was my friends here at the mall that brought me back to life. They would pick me up, and I would come walking with them, and slowly I recovered.' The thought of this makes me feel strangely cheered.

'We coffee together when we're done walking,' she said, 'And we have a birthday club, with cake, treats and gifts,' she added, nodding to herself. 'We're a family,' she finishes.

It's plain to me as that these dear souls have formed a bond at a time of life when loss and loneliness can threaten to darken the rest of their days.

NORTH DAKOTA

And so it's goodbye Minnesota and hello North Dakota. If you like fields, and all things udderly, this is the place for you. Milk is the official state drink. It's home to Salem Sue, the world's biggest fibreglass cow, and Dakota Thunder, the world's largest concrete buffalo.

From my carriage window there's little to break the horizon line apart from the cattle and a relatively new feature of the landscape: the oil pump. It's something that once inspired hope, but has now come to mark quite the opposite in what is the least visited state in America. But that's no excuse to ride on through, in my opinion. When you're touring America, trying to understand what makes the country tick, you can't expect to uncover it all at Disneyland.

Dakota Thunder, the world's largest concrete buffalo.

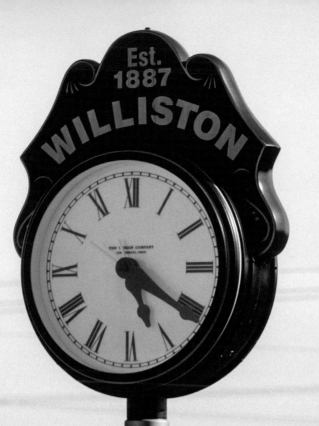

WILLISTON'S WOES: FROM BOOM TOWN TO BUST

Williston is not going to win any prizes as a tourist attraction. Then again, it was only recently that people flocked here not to see the sights but to seek their fortunes. It's one of those wee places that radically changed overnight. This quiet farming town had a population of about ten thousand, until oil was discovered and fracking transformed everything.

Now fracking almost seems like a swear word to me, you know? 'Get your feet off the fracking table!' That's how I think of it, rather than a means of getting gas and oil out of the ground using chemicals, sand and water. It's work that's both physically demanding and dangerous, which means it's well paid. And large pay packets will attract people from far and wide in huge numbers.

In Williston, during the oil boom, the population trebled to thirty thousand. For a town that previously relied on farming to survive, it must've seemed like a blessing. Now, some people consider it to be a curse they could've avoided.

Fracking is a controversial topic. Some believe it's the future, and a way to stop being so reliant on importing energy supplies. Critics say that it can mess with the water table and blame the practice for cases where it's been turned completely toxic. Whatever your view, it seems like a crime against the earth to me. I know I'm supposed to be neutral, but that's neither here nor there. The thoughts of an ageing hippy count for nothing when there's millions of dollars at stake. And people did make money here. At the same time, as demand rose so too did rents. All well and fine when people are flush, but then came the global slump in oil prices and Williston was left with its pants down.

As the *Empire Builder* approaches the station, I'm not sure what I'll find. On the road just outside town I spot a huge sign welcoming visitors to 'Boomtown USA', but something tells me that might be a little misleading.

'Oh, boy, there's no other place like it right now,' says a softly spoken guy in a store when I stop for a bottle of water (I didn't fancy a drink out of the tap). 'At one point we had eight people per day moving into town; coming off the train with their backpacks and suitcases. All of them looking for that one chance – maybe their last chance – and not so long ago they found that chance right here.'

It's a strangely upbeat welcome, but he leaves a great deal unspoken. The very fact that it's so quiet back on the street speaks volumes. In many ways, it feels like a place straight out of the Wild West, with its station, its parade of shops and its benches. What's missing are the people, but like any cowboy new in town I definitely get the sense that my presence has been noted.

For a moment, I stand and check out the store fronts. It's a downtrodden sight, for sure. Across the street is a bar that rejoices in the wonderful name of No Place. A closer inspection of the welcoming sign tells me this is a bar that 'welcomes bikers'. What does that tell you about the clientele we might find inside? Well let me tell you one thing for free. I'm not going in there to find out, that's for sure too.

A little further down stand two strip joints. Neon piping spells out the names of each, but the lure of the glow is lost in the blazing sunlight. No doubt during the boom time, the girls inside would be dancing on poles having ten- and twenty-dollar notes shoved into their bikini bottoms. Then the slump comes and they find their knickers are full of small change. What really stands out for me is the fact that neighbouring these joints is a Salvation Army centre. I have a feeling they might be busy and decide to find out for myself.

'We hope to bring light to the darkness in this community,' Captain Josh tells me, a portly man standing proud in his uniform. Behind him, among those gathered in the little waiting room, I spot a man asleep on a plastic chair. He sits there with his arms folded and head dropped back. He looks exhausted but not from physical work, I think to myself. 'In a sad way,' Josh continues, 'this is our boom time.'

I spot administrative staff at work in an office behind the lobby. They look busy.

'Were you here before the oil?' I ask.

'A few years ahead of the boom,' he says. 'But now we're into the slow-down period with the oil price dropping. People have lost their jobs, and often that means their homes as well. Sometimes it happens very quickly. We're talking over a twenty-four-hour period. So they're in a hard place, trying to figure out how to get home, or just find a roof over their heads, and that's when many come here.'

When the good times came to an abrupt end, I learn, the supermarket car park became an impromptu dorm for men sleeping in their pick-ups. And as we all know, when there are too many men, things can get stupid, violent and unpleasant pretty quickly. Things calmed down as people packed up and left town, while many of those who remain appear to have nowhere else to go. What really distresses me about this story is that the sky-high rents haven't dropped, despite the slump. I guess there's still enough oil work to keep the housing sector happy, but that will come as no comfort to those who find themselves on skid row. It must be miserable, especially because in wintertime the temperature here can drop to eighteen degrees below.

'What are the chances of finding further employment in Williston?' I ask, seeking some silver lining.

'Slim,' reports Captain Josh. 'Most people think we're in for another rough year, with more layoffs before we see any improvement. The economy is just so uncertain and everyone is affected by it. We just do what we can to help with the resources we have.' Josh invites me to check out the centre's chapel. I follow him, wondering what it must be like to walk in here with no hope and find someone like this saint of a man and his blessed team, willing to help no matter what. 'We used to see twenty-five cases each week,' he tells me from the aisle of the chapel. 'Now we deal with that figure every day. For our first winter, we effectively just opened up as a heating centre. A place for people to come and just be warm. We'd give them a blanket and they'd settle into the pews here for a couple of hours.'

Humbled, I say nothing for a moment.

'Do you ever help people to get home?' I ask finally.

'Oh, yeah. All the time.' Josh nods and smiles, as if welcoming the question. They come here, having been out of work for a month or two. They're trying their hardest, and doing what they can to survive, and sometimes just accepting that it's time to leave is the bravest decision they can make.'

'How do the local people cope with the situation?' I ask.

'Many of them have also moved away,' he says. 'A minority were upset with us because we're helping people new to this town, but our mission is to provide help where there's need. We're a faith-based organisation, but people don't have to believe to come here. We're simply here to help, wherever you're from.'

I look around the chapel. It's modern, plain and, I imagine, well attended when Josh and his wife hold their service every Sunday.

'Who preaches?' I ask him.

'We take turns.' He shows me the instruments behind the lectern. 'My wife also plays the guitar and sings. I play the drums so I don't have to sing.'

'Or take part in the music,' I suggest.

'Nobody wants to hear me do that,' he agrees, before inviting me through an unassuming door to one side of the chapel. Following him into a well-lit space, I find myself faced by a mountain of boxes.

'This is our food pantry,' says Josh. 'When people come in, they sign up and get a box.'

It's overwhelming, in many ways, to think what demand there must be behind a space chock-full of basic supplies. There's a guy in here hard at work packing up boxes at a table. He's wearing overalls with the sleeves rolled up to the elbows and has dedication written all over his face. This is Gordy, Josh says by way of introduction. A lifelong Williston resident and loyal volunteer. I shake hands, with just one question on my mind.

'Do you hate the oil men?'

It's a little direct, I know, but someone has to take responsibility for this desperate situation. Gordy shrugs in response.

'It's nice working with Captain Josh,' is all he says.

It would be the easiest thing in the world to put the boot into Williston, but one thing it does speak well of is the inherent can-do spirit of Americans. This is a nation built on immigrants, after all, who weren't afraid to pack up and move on if they had to, and that spirit is still here. It's not just in those who came here to work on the oilfields, either. Leaving the Sally Ann centre behind, some of the crew bumped into a taxi owner awaiting a fare whose story had to be told. She was drawn to move to the town during the good times, she said, because things had got so bad for her back home.

'It was basically the money,' admits Sheila Taranto, a slim, blonde and very striking seventy-year-old grandmother in a duck-billed cap. 'Things were falling apart in Alaska, where I'm from, and I'd heard a lot of stories about Williston.'

'All good?' One of the team asks, and Sheila laughs.

'The things I heard scared me off for about two years because a woman on her own at my age . . . what's she going to do? Well I knew what I'd do,' she follows up quickly and levels her gaze at them. 'I was going to come here and start a cab company!'

Sheila has the kind of bright smile that must be lovely to glimpse in the rear-view mirror when you're chatting to her from the back seat of her cab. But what drew her into this line of work?

'Well, it just seemed to be my talent in life,' she says. 'I'd run a cab service back home for twenty-seven years, from the Arctic to Wasilla, Anchorage and the Aleutian Islands. I was always very successful at it and the men never scared me. I knew the money was here in Williston with the oilfields, and you know, I'm getting a little older and it might be my last time. So, I figured despite the bad stuff in the media I'd see if I could do it all over again.'

Even the bad stuff?

Sheila shrugs, not dropping that charming smile.

'Well, there was a lot of drinking,' she says, and pauses. 'I think it depends on what side of the fence you play on, and I'm always real careful,' she says instead. 'I just figured if I didn't go to North Dakota to see what it's like I'd never know. So, one day after I had all the housekeeping done, I just packed up and said if I can't make it I can always drive back.'

And what did you find when you arrived?

'Well, they just didn't have the law enforcement,' she says, like her audience should be able to read between the lines. 'This is where all the end-of-the-world type of characters come, sort of like the Klondike. So, a lot of the people I met were the ones that burn every bridge along their way in getting here. They said it was the only place in America they could have felonies and get a job.'

I am really impressed when I hear about the encounter by Sheila's drive and courage, as well as her single-minded determination to make her mark in the town.

So, how did the cab company get off the ground?

'First thing, I went to the city council to see if it was possible to get a taxi permit. I'd heard all this rumbling that there wasn't a good service in the area, and it turned out I was right. They awarded me the opportunity, and here I am. I started out with one car and that multiplied to six during the boom. For three years it was very prosperous and then all the drilling stopped.'

Sheila halts here, but the team tell me they could see in her eyes how the rest of her story played out before she continued.

'Twenty-six thousand people were laid off almost immediately,' she says, which is an unimaginable number. 'A lot of the rigs shut down. When I got here, we had two hundred and thirteen operating in the field. Now it's down to sixty-eight.'

Despite this being such a tough tale, Sheila continues to beam – a beacon of hope.

'The way I see it, life is less stressful since I got rid of all the boyfriends and the husbands,' she says. 'So, I'm going to keep going for another five years. Together with the bartender, it's always the cab driver that's the last to leave town. I'm gonna stick things out, and hope that it comes back,' she says. And I hope that she thrives no matter what, and wish I could tell her that in person. Sheila's story leaves no doubt about her confidence. 'Unless we change our supply of energy, and go to nuclear or something from outer space,' she says, 'we still need oil.'

It strikes me when I hear this story that I have visited a town of deep contrasts. There is doom, gloom and despair on every street corner, but also pockets of hope, and without that we'd all be finished. No doubt there will be better times ahead, but so much of that original town has been destroyed in the process. I just hope the people like what they get, because when that much money has been invested in something it'll be there for a long time.

Back on board the train, as we leave the station behind I find myself plucking out a tune on my banjo. As I find my way, I begin to sing a wee ditty that quite possibly makes sense only to me – and to those who once sought their fortunes in this town.

Take me back to Williston, I want to be fracking again.
I want to be fracking again, ohhh, I wanna be fracking again.
Oh, take me back to Williston, I want to be fracking again,
I want to be fracking again and again and again.
Cos I'm an oil guy, an oil guy,
And I've been away from Williston and I don't miss it one bit.

4

MONTANA

1

'I love your glasses,' a lady said to me that night on the train. 'You know, you look like Billy Connolly?'

I said: 'I do know,' with the straightest face I could muster, and we chatted for a wee while. Travelling by train is a great leveller, I think. There are no airs and graces, unless you're locked away in First Class. With the passing of time measured by the mile, people use the opportunity to just talk to one another, and I love that.

Beneath an epic cloudscape, we're crossing a terrain that was once considered to be the ultimate land of plenty. With its forested valleys, rivers and prairie grasslands, cradled by snow-capped mountains, the state of Montana was effectively regarded as a Garden of Eden when first discovered. Fishermen were said to land a catch simply by throwing a basket into the waters. Grouse were so numerous you could creep up on them while they slept, pop them under your arm and take them home for the pot. The settlers who first arrived here must've thought they'd landed in heaven on earth. And they'd been through hell to get here, travelling by horse and cart, or simply on foot. Can you imagine that? The distance is incredible. Many fell ill or suffered injuries or attack along the way and didn't make it. All this goes through my mind as I look out of the carriage window. It really is a magnificent view, something so many don't appreciate about this country, and I'm fired up with excitement at the next stop on my cross-country trek. On a map, as we close in on our next destination, I feel like I'm revisiting my roots.

HOME FROM HOME: IN THE COMPANY OF GLASGOWNIANS

This is Glasgow, but there are no docks here, or persistent drizzle. It's a ranching town in the heart of Montana's rolling plains. Now, the reason it got the name was down to James Hill, who built the railway from Chicago to Seattle. He decided to have a little stopover here, and pondering what to call the place he spun a globe, stuck his finger out at random and it stopped at Glasgow. And that's how the next town got to be called Malta. Pretty good, huh? I wouldn't be surprised to find Swaziland a couple of miles up the road.

There's nothing brash about this railroad town. It's functional and clean, with no excess of stores, and ultimately here to serve the farming community. I make my way to the local radio station because I've heard there's a show going on right now that intrigues me. Do you remember *Swap Shop* from the Eighties? It sounds a little bit like that, but with bigger skies and thick American accents.

'Well, hello-o-o,' chirps station manager Shirley, a silver-headed force of nature who grabs me for a kiss on the cheek. 'We have matching hair!' she chuckles, and she's right.

It takes me a moment to grasp that I haven't so much walked into a wee radio building as into a shrine to Elvis Presley. There are pictures and paraphernalia everywhere. On every shelf and wall space, the King reigns supreme.

'There must be a reason for this?' I say, as Shirley takes me on a tour.

'In 1958, when I was a little girl, Elvis came through on the *Empire Builder*,' she explains. 'We stood up on the platform chanting, "We want Elvis! We want Elvis!"'

'And did you get Elvis?'

'We never even saw him,' she says, and begins to hoot so heartily it's clear the irony still isn't lost on her after nearly fifty years.

Over the next few minutes, she delights in showing me everything from Elvis-themed thimbles and cuckoo clocks to tissue holders, cookie jars and butter knives. I am very happy indeed to be sidetracked from the purpose of my visit, which is to inspect her collection. I love Elvis as much as anyone, but perhaps not quite as much as Shirley does. By the time she breaks off from taking me through her line-up of Russian Presley dolls and introduces me to Hayley, the radio presenter, I've almost forgotten why I'm here.

'We're about to go on air with the *Tradeo* show,' she says, and that's quite enough to refocus my attention. 'It's an interesting animal,' she goes on to explain as we take our seats in the studio. 'Someone might phone in with a vehicle they want to sell, for example, and we'll give their number to any listener who is interested. People from cities gasp when they hear that we're doing this, but in Glasgow everyone knows each other. They're not strangers.'

'That's the great thing about small towns,' I agree. 'Some might feel it's claustrophobic, but isn't this kind of connection what societies are built on?'

'We help trade everything,' Hayley tells me, having introduced the show, name-checked its sponsors and then promised to be right back after a song track. 'Last week a lady successfully sold her corrective pantyhose.'

This amuses me greatly, though it's a very different sort of intimate item that the first caller offers up.

'A bunny rabbit?' I ask, to clarify when we cut for another song. 'A real live one?'

'We get a lot of animals,' says Hayley, who goes on to negotiate a lift across town for a puppy from the next call to come in.

When we finally get to goods that don't have a face or a mother, I discover that the people of Glasgow, Montana, are willing to trade anything from inexpensive chest freezers to a love seat that only needs a little cleaning to be as good as new. It makes for fascinating listening and provides an illuminating focus on what makes a small community tick.

'What do you call yourselves?' I ask Hayley, during a couple of words from the sponsors. 'Are you Glaswegians?'

'We're more Glasgownian,' she tells me, and I like the sound of that a lot.

Watching Hayley at work in front of the microphone, it's clear she loves her job. It's like watching human glue at work: binding people together by helping to shift unwanted items to loving homes. As the show draws to an end, she asks me where I'm visiting next. I tell her I'm heading for a cattle ranch across town.

'I know who you're meeting,' she tells me, which is no surprise to me at all, and also wonderfully heartening. 'You'll be very well looked after.'

On my way out of the studio, leaving Hayley to press on finding homes for kittens and coffee tables, Shirley grabs me to show me some final items from her treasured collection.

'A velvet Elvis,' I say, because there's no other way to describe the framed patchwork portrait in front of me. 'Or is it a Velvis?'

Shirley's laughter fills the little hallway. Then she invites me to try on her sequinned Elvis coat that she only ever wears on his birthday. It's an honour and also a challenge when a man in my condition is asked to give his finest Elvis shakedown. I do my level best, which isn't great, but my host's lovely chuckle leaves me feeling like the king of the world.

'You want to stay, don't you?' she says when we finally reach the exit doors, and it sounds like she's read my mind.

I turn to face her. Still laughing, as if she might never stop, Shirley spreads her arms for a hug. I think I've fallen in love.

WHEN THE GOING GETS TOUGH: THE LAST OF THE COWBOYS

Hayley is quite right about my next encounter. I am very well looked after. Even before we arrive at his ranch, I want to phone in and tell her that Lee is indeed great company. On the journey out of Glasgow in my host's wagon, bumping along tracks straight out of *The Dukes of Hazzard*, we listen to the *Tradeo* show on the radio and talk about this well-respected cattle man's life and times.

'I've got a lot of memories here,' says Lee, a man in a chequered shirt and cowboy hat with the brim pulled low, gum in his mouth and a moustache you could only get away with if you knew how to handle a bucking bronco. Quite simply, Lee *looks* like a rancher from the top of his head to his cowboy boots. He smells like a rancher, he sounds like a rancher and he shares the

kind of wisdom that only a rancher could possess. Earlier, Lee told me the names of fifteen kinds of grass. I didn't know that many existed. I thought there was grass and no grass. 'Yup. Been right here for sixty-four years,' he continues. 'Spent four of them at college, and when I graduated it was like getting out of jail.'

Even before he tells me this, Rancher Lee strikes me as a man who has learned everything from the school of life.

'Did you have plans?' I ask as I'm bounced about in my seat.

'All I ever wanted to do was this,' he says before telling me how his mother insisted he attend classes. 'She told me I couldn't come back here unless I went somewhere and got an education, and I was still scared of her so I went.'

Minutes later, the entrance to our destination comes into view. The Cornwell Ranch has been here since 1892. Not that there are any buildings visible. It's just arable land as far as I can see. Lee drives through the gates, taking us underneath the giant iron head of a steer suspended from a frame. I suspect a lot of beef has been produced here and Lee is plainly very proud of what generations of his family have achieved.

'I think probably my heritage goes back to England or Wales or somewhere over that way,' he tells me. 'I don't know whether the King ran our family out of the country or whether they came over here voluntarily, or what happened.' Lee keeps his eyes on the road as he talks. 'We never researched it back any farther,' he goes on. 'But I think rather than being descended from royalty we're probably descended from hillbillies in West Virginia.'

We share a chuckle. I haven't even looked the man in the eye just yet, but I like him enormously.

'There's an honour in being chucked out of a place,' I suggest.

Lee shifts up a gear and agrees. We might be on family land now, but the ranch house is still nowhere in sight. It's just a long, winding dirt road across grassland studded with handsome-looking cattle. As we rock over potholes, Lee explains how it was the age of the train that transformed the landscape and provided a livelihood for families like his.

'The railroad was put through here in 1887,' he tells me. 'My grandfather came out from West Virginia. He was in the sheep business till 1948. Since then, we've always been cattle.'

'How many do you have now?' I ask, well aware that I can see cows as far as the horizon.

'This year, we've branded about forty-five hundred.'

Lee rolls out this figure like he might've done them all in a day.

'That's a lot,' I say.

'Well, there's a lot of us,' he says, and finally looks around to flash me a smile. 'We're like mice. It takes a lot of hands and a lot of backs to make it all go forward, you know?'

A moment later, as our conversation turns to just how much land is required to keep so many cattle, Lee pulls up and invites me to feel the wind on my face.

'Can you imagine bringing your bride out here?' he asks, as we stand beside the wagon and admire the wide open plain. 'You've just got a hundred and sixty acres or even three hundred and twenty acres of land from the Federal Government for the filing fee, and you go to the railroad and pick her up. She's all excited, and so you bring her out here and go "Honey, we're home!"'

I try to picture my wife's face as he says this. Lee and I are laughing, but somehow I doubt she'd find it funny.

'It must've been hard,' I say, and I'm not just thinking about placating a murderous-looking missus.

Lee adopts a philosophical tone.

'Y'know, this is as good as it gets. You could choose to plough up the land, but a lot of years you wouldn't get your seed back if it failed to rain at the right time. Things were a lot tougher in those days than they are now, but it was still an opportunity to own something of your own. You just couldn't be faint of heart if you wanted to survive.'

'The winters,' I think out loud. 'How is it then?'

Lee faces me side on.

'It can kill you,' he says. 'Some days it will be twenty to thirty below and the wind will be blowing. We just keep the cattle moving through the year. In April, the cows calve in the pastures. Then we move them up to these parts before making a circle at the north end of the ranch and starting back. It's kind of like a migration. An unending process – you just gotta keep going.'

Back in the truck, we move forward to the 1930s, when drought and the Great Depression turned America's farming landscape into a dustbowl.

'I feel sad for those who had to give it up back then,' I say.

'Well, the ones that came here had an agricultural background,' says Lee, as if seeking some silver lining from that tragic tale. 'They knew that if they could just plant a garden, raise a bunch of vegetables and potatoes, have some chickens and a milk cow, they could make it through, you know? It didn't take a lot of cash.'

I tell him that just from looking around it's clear his family must have that skill in spades.

'We're all homesteaders,' he says, and I love that term. 'When my grandfather was ready to get rid of the ranch he just split it up amongst his kids and then two of them got to buy everyone else out. That's how it happened and then my brothers and I got the same kind of deal going. They've both passed away, but I've got two nephews, two nieces, a son and a daughter who are all involved in the ranch here, besides my generation.'

'A family affair,' I say, nodding to myself.

What happens next brings the story alive in my mind. Just as I'm wondering whether Lee's kids will stick at it, with so many other opportunities available in this day and age, he pulls the wagon off the track and heads across even bumpier terrain.

'The second winter, around 1893, my grandfather and his partner on the ranch moved up here because there was a bunch of grass in these hills where they could keep the sheep. So, they made a dugout in the ground and this is where they lived.'

Lee pulls up ahead of a depression in the ground just in front of a gentle slope. It's covered in long grass, but I can't say what variety it is.

IT'S WHAT'S
FOR DINNER

'Is this it?' I ask, wondering how Lee's grandfather could once have called it 'home'. I can see some kind of structure might once have stood here, but it must've been pretty desperate.

'They shovelled out the dirt, built up walls with logs and thatched a roof with brush,' says Lee.

'My God!'

Rancher Lee revels in my astonishment. I expect everyone who works here knows all about fortitude in the face of adversity. It leaves me feeling like I'm in the company of a far hardier species than me.

'They had one pair of shoes between them,' Lee adds, as if life hadn't been tough enough for the poor bastards. 'So the one that went out with the sheep took the shoes and the other wore sacks around his feet and stayed in the dugout.'

It sounds like torture. In their shoes, whether or not it was my turn, I'd have thrown in the towel within hours.

'How did they manage?' I wonder.

'They had wood for heat and an axe,' says Lee. 'There was probably water in the creek where they could melt snow, and jack rabbits and deer to eat. So they must have had enough to make it through the winter.' He catches my eye. 'Or I wouldn't be here,' he admits.

'Me neither.'

'You could say it's a tribute to persistence.' Lee plunges his hands in his pockets, his gaze fixed on what was once a shelter. 'Yup.'

In the world of cattle and sheep ranching here in the Treasure State, so called because of Montana's rich mineral deposits, it isn't just the elements that can threaten livelihoods. During my time in Lee's company, his tone would darken considerably at the very mention of coyotes. I wanted to find out more about what is clearly an uneasy relationship between ranchman and beastie. So, with a brisk wind gathering over the prairies, I set off to speak to a local legend in controlling Montana's most infamous pest.

TRUE SHOT: THE LIFE AND TIMES OF GENE ETCHART

For a figure that has earned a reputation across the state as a revered huntsman, I half expected to find our man in a manor house and surrounded by wall-mounted busts of stuffed animals. In reality, Gene Etchart shares a delightfully modest suburban bungalow with his wife. For a man in his senior years, Gene is softly spoken, outwardly laconic but pin-sharp when it comes to retelling his experiences stalking coyote across Montana.

'We had a situation here where a good part of the hard work that our farmers and ranchers were doing was going down the drain because of the coyotes,' he tells me, before explaining how the lambs and calves are vulnerable to predators. 'So there was a market for someone to thin them out, and that's when I stepped in.'

Gene may not look like a man who can take a tin can off a wall at two hundred paces, but he boasts a formidable record. Not just for picking off coyotes

Gene may not look like a man who can take a tin can off a wall at two hundred paces, but he boasts a formidable record. Not just for picking off coyotes throughout a long career, but also for doing so from the air.

throughout a long career, but also for doing so from the air. When you consider the sheer size of the landscape, it's no surprise to learn that he took to the skies with his rifle. On arriving at his home, I came across a photograph of him standing in a hangar surrounded by the dead beasts.

'It looks like fifty or sixty,' I say.

'One hundred ten,' he says to correct me – this, quite clearly from a man with an eye for accuracy. 'Before the helicopters, when we got a coyote we had to run him down by propeller plane. And if he was out in rough badland country we had to find a place to land and remove the skin from the body.'

'For the pelts?'

'Absolutely. For the value of their furs.'

'How many would you get in a day?' I ask.

'I would say that probably an average would be six or seven. Nowadays you'll be getting a hundred with the helicopter.'

I consider what would make a chopper advantageous when it came to hunting coyote. Gene tells me it all comes down to the increased precision and control at the pilot's disposal.

'In an airplane you're doing seventy miles an hour when you fly over your target. A coyote is running at about thirty miles an hour, so the airplane and the shot that comes out of the gun are both travelling faster than the coyote. It means you don't aim for the head but just behind the tail. That way the shot will catch up.'

'That's extraordinary.' I can barely comprehend how much concentration it must take to be lining up a target in the cross hairs from the side of a speeding aircraft. As well as the marksman, I figure it must take some precision from the pilot, too.

'Some of the hunters rigged up their planes so they could fly alone,' Gene tells me, which makes my mind boggle. 'Mostly we went up in pairs and took turns behind the controls.'

'D'you know, I had no idea that coyotes were such a nuisance,' I say.

'They can take out ten per cent of your livestock,' Gene tells me. 'When you're sitting down with your banker and he says your income is down ten per cent, it could be the difference between a profit and a loss, or even moving on to another business.'

When he tells me that your average rancher might own ten thousand sheep, it's clear the coyote's taste for lamb suppers can come at a high price.

'When did you learn to shoot and fly?' I ask, because I'm wondering what came first: the pilot's licence or the pest control job?

'Well that's a darned good question,' he says, though in the pause that follows I can't be sure he's going to answer it. 'You know when I was growing up as a little boy on a farm, I had a .22 rifle,' he continues finally. 'I'd go around shooting gophers or ground squirrels, but once in a while I'd hear the throb of an airplane. It's just like a kid nowadays wants to be a fireman or something, I knew that's what I wanted to do. Many years later, when the time came that I'd earned forty dollars, I headed over to the airport, ran up to a plane that had just landed and asked the pilot for lessons.'

I realise I am grinning from ear to ear when he shares this with me. It's fair to say that world has gone where you can walk up to a pilot and he'll teach you how to fly.

'So were you the first to offer your services as an aerial coyote hunter?'

Gene shrugs, which leaves me none the wiser.

'We had an old aviator here that flew for a doctor, a kind of a pleasure airplane. Once I'd got my basic licence, I helped him circulate a sort of petition around to the sheep men that if they would pay somebody five dollars a piece for legitimate evidence of a kill then I could be of service.' This was a fair price, he tells me when I ask him about it. 'Every time I killed a coyote their income went up a little bit.'

'Did it make you rich?'

Once again, Gene replies in his own fashion. It's charming to hear, and evidence that money wasn't the sole motivation of this man with a passion for flight.

No doubt the coyotes watched my noble ride threading westwards. I doubt very much that any of them thought they had just a dodged a bullet.

'I told this old aviator that if he let me take the controls and taught me the tricks, I'd fly him low so he could shoot at coyote. And if he took one out he got paid for that, while I earned time in my logbook.'

'It sounds like the perfect job share,' I say, delighted by the sound of this arrangement.

'Well, after about three years of that, and more advanced flying, I took the tests and became a professional commercial flying instructor.'

Gene Etchart is ninety-six now and still likes to fly. He even offered to take me up in his plane for the sheer pleasure of a spin. It was a kind offer, though I declined politely. I had a train to catch, I told him, but between ourselves I was nervous about placing my life in the hands of a man his age. He's a lovely guy who offered me a window into a world that's long gone now, what with the choppers doing all the dirty work. But frankly, despite his decades of experience my appreciation of his talent just didn't stretch that far. I worried he'd whack the machine into reverse at some point and give me a heart attack. Back on board the *Empire Builder*, I knew I had already found the most agreeable way to travel across this spectacular state. No doubt the coyotes watched my noble ride threading westwards. I doubt very much that any of them thought they had just a dodged a bullet.

FORT PECK LAKE: WATER WORLD

Before we get out of Dodge – or Montana, as it should be known – I want to make a few more stops. There's so much to enjoy here, after all. First on my list is a stretch of water that I hear every visitor should see. Even though we're in a landlocked state, it's a prospect that hardly sets my heart aflutter. It's only when we reach a vantage point that overlooks my destination that I appreciate what all the fuss is about. Yes, it's a lake, and we've all seen plenty of those, but this one stands out from all the rest for one very good reason: it's entirely manmade.

This is Fort Peck Lake, not far from Glasgow, and it's a miracle. That humans are responsible for what looks like a sea to my eye is astonishing. The lake was created in the 1930s, along with Fort Peck Dam, and stretches over one hundred and thirty miles along the course of the Missouri River. It's only the fifth-largest lake in the United States, but the fact that it wouldn't exist at all without vision, blood, sweat and tears is truly humbling.

I've always been a great fan of anything built by human hands. It's like when you go to Rome and feel a sense of pride for your species when you see what they built and achieved, you know? Or you visit the Great Pyramids and think, Oh my God, you can say it was aliens till you're blue in the earlobes, but I think these were built by human beings who were just dead clever. The tragedy is those clever people are almost always then killed by oafs. Because it seems to me civilisation reaches a certain pitch, and creates something truly wonderful, only for rumblings to gather strength from behind the hills as the oafs approach, hell-bent on wrecking things.

Fortunately, nobody has wrecked the lake or the dam at Fort Peck. It was Franklin D. Roosevelt's commitment to tackling the unemployment problem by sweeping people into the countryside to do great things that is largely responsible for the creation of this awe-inspiring reservoir. For a long time, I think, Roosevelt hasn't received due recognition for his achievements, and this seals it for me. It took up to forty thousand people to dig this big hole, all of them descending on a little town with just two hundred and fifty residents. What they created has a coastline longer than California, and when they were

finished they upped sticks and sought their fortunes elsewhere. Just take a moment to think about that. Incredible, eh?

When I stand at the water's edge and look out, the far side is little more than a pencil trace. The lake is immense, and it's hard to imagine that anyone thought such a huge undertaking was even possible to pull off. That's why I love people, and I'm pleased I came to what is quite a desolate spot to see such an understated wonder of the world. Say what you like about Roosevelt, he deserves a pat on the back for his hand in this. In a way, it takes the polar opposite of today's career politicians to make things like this happen and involve the people in the process. It's quite frightening, and I think now more

than ever we need the driven type of politician: the seer who can see the future and is willing to stand up, take the ridicule and fight for it. There's not been many of their kind. James Maxton was a great Scotsman in that respect. There's also John Maclean and Rory Gallagher, but such characters seem to have disappeared. There's not enough people ready to kick arse. I think now even more than in the past we need somebody who's willing to speak for the earth and for the working man.

While I'm in such a rosy mood about Roosevelt, we mustn't forget he was responsible for another great achievement: the old age pension. That must've made Americans very happy. So happy, in fact, they wrote a wee song about it.

When the old age pension check comes through the door
Dear old grandpa won't be lonesome any more
Every night he'll have a date, he'll be waiting at the gate
When the old age pension check comes through the door.

I sing it to myself from the shoreline, pause to reflect in the silence and then dissolve into laughter. My poor film crew. Here I am intending to provide an insight into the history of the lake and the dam and I've transformed the moment into a musical. Next thing they know, people will be crowding in from the wings to sing the chorus. I think it might be time I got back in my box on rails.

SO, A LION WALKS INTO A GLAZING STORE . . . SMALL TOWN, BIG LEGEND

In 1891, the railway company dropped off a boxcar here and called it Shelby Junction. There was no town here at the time. You could just name places willy-nilly in those days, and so the railroad workers chose to honour their manager, Peter Shelby. Shelby, though, seemed singularly unimpressed. When he came to visit what is still the most remote station on the Amtrak network, he took one look and declared, 'It's a mud hole of a goddamn place and won't come to anything.'

Nothing much happened after that, which threatened to prove Peter Shelby right. Then, in 1921, some local Jack the Lads conspired to hold up a train. An opera company was on board. They were on tour at the time, but this kind of performance wasn't part of the schedule. The gang, who had guns, shot out the train's headlamp and forced it to stop. So far so average when it comes to true crime, you might think, but wait until you hear what happens next. Because as well as relieving the opera company and the rest of the passengers of their valuables, the robbers earned their place in local folklore by ordering the guard onto the side of the track in order to perform a clog dance. Methinks there wasn't much to do in Shelby at the time.

Like so many small towns, years could pass with very little happening of note, only for something so monumentally unpredictable to occur that everyone talks about it for decades to come. So fast-forward with me to 1996. Then, Shelby's peace and tranquillity were shattered when a mountain lion charged into a double-glazing store.

When I first heard about this historic event, I could only think Shelby must be cold in winter if a lion had come looking for a way to keep his den warm. I can't offer you much more than that, not while keeping a straight face, but I was thrilled to be able to speak to the owner of the double-glazing store. We may not be getting the story straight from the lion's mouth, for he's now stuffed and mounted in the visitors' centre down the street, but it's the next-best thing. She was there, after all.

'The hair just stood up on the back of my neck,' says Jeanne McDonough, who was alone in her little store downtown that August when her unexpected customer showed up in such dramatic fashion. She's a warm, friendly lady, and instantly likeable. Jeanne must've told this tale many times over, yet she recounts it for me with aplomb as if it happened yesterday. 'I was just sitting in the back doing my books when I heard this terrific crash. We have a little walkway through from the entrance. I came out, heard people in the street screaming and then I laid eyes on the lion. It was kind of dazed-looking, having just crashed through the glass.'

'It must've been quite a shock,' I say, thinking not just for Jeanne but for the lion too.

'I just beelined it back,' she continues. 'Our dogs were freaking out, and I realised that had I been out there at the time it would've run straight into me.'

'You're lucky to be alive.'

Jeanne laughs, but it's true.

If I came face to face with a lion, I'd say there's a very high chance that only one of us would live to tell the tale, and it probably wouldn't be me. But what I love about her story is the fact that news travels fast in a place like this.

Within minutes people were saying, 'Hey, come on down to the double-glazing store, there's a lion in there!' Jeanne's cowering for her life while kids are gathering on the sidewalk astride their bikes, gawping. Now, I wouldn't be too happy to see so many wee children there, and I imagine Jeanne was pretty relieved when the police and the rangers showed up. When I ask her, Jeanne takes a more philosophical view.

'In the middle of a small town, in the middle of a prairie, and in the middle of my store, I figured if I got eaten by a mountain lion, then it was *my* time to go.'

Fortunately for Jeanne, who managed to get out, it was a happy outcome for her. Not so for the lion, as I just mentioned; though given the danger it presented to the public, plus its injuries, it was perhaps the most merciful option. But I now want to know if this was a one-off visit or a regular threat. Jeanne tells me that while lions are often sighted nearer the river and sometimes the occasional moose will go by the store – just window shopping, presumably – there's an even bigger visitor around town that she hopes *won't* get an urge to pop in.

'The grizzly bears have started coming off the mountains and passing through the prairie again,' she says. 'It's very unusual. Something must be happening up in the mountains to drive them down. We've certainly had an inordinate amount of forest fire, which has been stirring things up, so we need to be vigilant.'

Very kindly, Jeanne offers to take me to the visitors' centre so that I can see the great creature. I thought she'd never ask. As we trundle along, chatting about local issues, I hear the now familiar sound of an Amtrak train easing along the tracks through town. Jeanne glances over my shoulder, towards the level crossing, and waves.

'That's my son-in-law,' she says, and points out a figure in the driver's cabin. 'They're good employers for us around here.'

I'm well aware that without the train there would be no Shelby. It's heartening to know that town and rail have such a close relationship.

Arriving at the centre, I learn that Jeanne has her own key. I wonder if this is a gift afforded to all the locals. I'm about to ask, but the sign on the door tickles me to distraction. NO PETS, it reads, which is a little late in the day, I think.

'My God,' I say, when I spot the beastie on display. I can't miss it. There's a sign introducing Shelby the Cat. It's clearly named after the town, but I'm not sure I would describe it as a cat. Certainly not one I'd be happy to keep in my house. It's huge, undeniably handsome, but with a ferocious glare that I imagine Jeanne will never forget.

'If you run into a grizzly they tend to turn around and take off,' she says. 'If a mountain lion crosses your path, chances are it's been stalking you for some time.'

Despite her close shave, we agree that it's a beautiful animal.

'But not so beautiful if it's on your back,' I point out.

'That's a whole different thing,' she says. 'I've learned that if you do run into one you're not supposed to back away because they'll just come after you. Instead,' she says, and spreads her arms wide, 'you open up your coat real big and make yourself seem larger than you are.'

Jeanne stops there, her focus drawn by the mountain lion once more. The glass case on a plinth puts them on a level here. There's no need to act big in its presence. Bound for evermore in the town's history by one rare encounter, it's as if the pair have learned to see eye to eye.

I have a little while before my train arrives in Shelby. Jeanne the lion lady told me she has not one but two sons-in-law who work as railroad drivers. So, if I'm lucky, I might get to meet the whole family. Until then, I have some time on my hands. Now, Shelby might be a small town, but if you poke about in places like this there's plenty to enjoy and it usually tells you a great deal. Take the large statue of two boxers belting seven shades out of each other. This commemorates the great world title fight between Jack Dempsey and Tommy Gibbons in 1923. It was a big deal and it happened right here in Shelby. With oil money flowing, local politicians decided they wanted to give the town a big name in the world. They got in touch with Dempsey's manager. He asked for three hundred thousand dollars and they said yes. Not only that. They shelled out another eighty-five thousand to build a stadium in the town. Shelby had just five hundred residents at the time and this shiny new venue had the capacity to hold forty thousand people! So Dempsey and Gibbons swept into town by train to a rapturous reception. Guys outside the stadium were selling tickets at fifty bucks for a ringside seat. You have to remember this was in the day when just a few dollars would buy you a good pair of shoes, so it's fair to say people were getting carried away.

Come the fight, everything was looking good. The bell went to mark the start of the first round, but before a punch was thrown the ticket sellers rushed in to see their heroes. Not about to ignore an opportunity, those who hadn't been able to afford a seat flocked in close behind and watched the fight for free. By all accounts, it was a dull event that Jack Dempsey, predictably, won. The main excitement came afterwards, when it was discovered that Dempsey's manager had made off with all the cash. As a result of the theft and the lost ticket sales, two local banks went to the wall and many local entrepreneurs lost everything. The stadium has long gone. A pizza restaurant stands in its place now. So I'm not entirely sure exactly what the statue of the two fighters commemorates. Still, it's an interesting thing to check out while you're munching on a slice of ham and pineapple.

As I head for the platform, having thoroughly enjoyed my wee stop-off in Shelby, I'm drawn to a nearby freight building by the sound of a lonesome cowboy singing of coyotes and cattle calls over an acoustic guitar. Whoever is behind it has a beautiful, velvety voice capable of switching from a deep baritone to a lilting yodel. It reminds me of Slim Whitman, and that's something I just can't ignore.

'It's the high plains style,' he tells me once he's through, and introduces himself as Wylie, simple as that.

'What does that mean, exactly?'

Wylie is leaning against the edge of the loading bay, guitar strapped over his shoulder and one boot pressed back against the frame. He's looking out across the tracks as the sun begins to set.

'Well,' he says, as if biding his time, 'we slow the tune way down and turn it into this ethereal thing. It aims to sum up the wide open spaces that you travel through up here. So that yodel you just heard works best when you're in the saddle some fifty miles from the nearest town.'

I nod to myself as he tells me this. It makes perfect sense. Just you and the horse and the wilderness, with nobody to tell you that you're singing out of key.

I ask Wylie if he'll play me something more. He responds with an old boxcar song by Jimmy Rogers, who was himself a railway worker as well a fabulous musician. A few bars in, a distant whistle signals the imminent arrival of the *Empire Builder*. It's so lovely. Not least because I know the tune. It's called 'Waiting for a Train'. And as the engine and the carriages rattle over the tracks, just feet from where we stand, I'm able to sing along with him at the top of my voice.

SEATTLE

As we close in on the end of this first leg of our journey, from east to west across the country, I feel enormously glad that we chose this mode of transport. We could've flown over the country in a matter of hours, and seen nothing. And though it's been a long haul I feel rested and content.

With a view of Puget Sound from my carriage window, glittering in the sun, I can see Seattle's skyline taking shape ahead. When the *Empire Builder* begins to slow, our guard addresses the passengers in a tone that suggests he's come to care for each and every one of us.

'By the way, if your friends and family are not there to greet you,' he concludes, having informed us that our last stop will be Quay Street Station, 'it's because you're early. And early is a good thing.'

THE SPACE NEEDLE: TO THE POINT

On arriving in any big city, it's easy to feel swallowed up. This is especially true if you've just spent a pleasant couple of days in small towns and wide-open spaces. So, in order to find some air, I head high.

A man called Chuckles Carlson co-designed the Seattle Space Needle. That's right. Chuckles Carlson. He doesn't sound much like an architect, does he? That's because he wasn't. He was head of a hotel chain. In 1961, attempting to dream up a figurehead for the World Fair the next year, he drew his vision

on the back of a beer mat. It's not often doodles end up as design classics, but with the help of an architect that's just what happened. It's an iconic building, and a familiar feature in Seattle. If you haven't seen it, imagine a flying saucer balanced on top of a fancy port decanter and you won't go far wrong. The disc structure at the top is in fact a restaurant with an observation deck atop. It stands six hundred and five feet high. I took the glass elevator to the summit, where a brisk wind can blow, whatever the weather.

I find myself looking down at one of the most popular places in America to move to. Seattle's a good town and everybody knows it. Lately, there's been a rush by Californians to live here. They want a better life for their children, and I can recognise the draw. You get the feeling that the people who live in Seattle are delighted to be here. That's a great sign, I feel. I'll tell you another thing. It rains a lot and they don't seem to mind. I can be moaning about the rain and they'll simply look up and go 'Oh yeah', as if you'd only just brought it to their attention. Maybe they could teach the world to ignore rain. An unusual talent, but it could cheer up the soggier nations no end.

Seattle was named after a Suquamish Indian chief. He lived on one of the little islands out in Puget Sound and went out of his way to make the settlers feel welcome. He sounds like a cheery kind of guy and that may have rubbed off on the residents, who strike me as being very happy human beings. In recognition of Chief Seattle's open-arms policy, his name now presides over a West Coast seaport with over half a million sunny inhabitants. Famous individuals born here include Jimi Hendrix, Bill Gates and Gypsy Rose Lee.

The more I learn about Chief Seattle, the more convinced I am he was a genius and years ahead of his time. Take this: 'What is a man without beasts? If all the beasts were gone, Man would die from a great loneliness of spirit, for what happens to the beasts soon happens to man. All things are connected.' Isn't that wonderful? But I tell you, he saved the best one for the subject of pollution: 'Whatever befalls the earth befalls the sons of the earth. If men spit upon the ground they spit upon themselves.' To the point, eh? Old Seattle knew what he was talking about. I don't know what he'd make of the tower, but now I've had a ponder from the top I'm taking myself off to see a citizen who resides below the waterline.

THE SEATTLE AQUARIUM: MR POTATO HEAD'S WATERY GRAVE

I've been here before. My daughter is mad keen on octopus and octopi. So we came here about a year ago to see Ink, the aquarium's most famous tentacle-toting resident. On that occasion, Ink was doing spectacular arm-and-leggy stuff. It was really quite something, you know? Making my way to his tank this time, I find to my crushing disappointment that he's asleep. Rather than performing like the wonder of nature that he is, Ink has suckered himself to the side of the glass for a snooze. Frankly, he looks more like snot hanging from a washing line, and that isn't so fancy.

Fortunately, help is at hand. Ink's handler, Catherine, is just preparing his lunch. She tells me that the prospect of food is sure to wake him and liven up the proceedings. Watching her get his meal ready, however, I can't help thinking it's going to traumatise some of the children who have gathered with me to watch. It isn't what Ink is about to eat that troubles me, which is basically a crabmeat mix. It's the vessel in which it'll be delivered.

'That's Mr Potato Head,' I say, as Catherine finishes stuffing the hollow plastic toy with Ink's lunch.

'Yes, it is,' she replies with a disarming smile, and I have no doubt its identity has been pointed out to her many times over.

Together with the children and their parents, with bated breath I watch Catherine ascend the ladder propped against the octopus tank. Using what looks like a pair of tongs, she lowers poor Mr Potato Head into the water. Now we see him clearly through the glass, that all-familiar face closing in on tentacles that begin to twitch and flex.

'It's like a Sixties horror film,' I say gleefully, and mimic what I think our plucky little guy would sound like pleading for help in the clutches of this monster of the deep. Then I think of the children and pipe down. Catherine, meanwhile, is entirely focused on making sure that Ink leaves nothing to waste.

'He's pretty good at picking out every last scrap,' she says, as yet more tentacles enfold the toy. As the octopus begins to rotate Mr Potato Head, I watch the toy's plug-in mouth and eyes sink to the bottom of the tank. 'All of his sucker discs are his taste buds,' Catherine explains. 'So everything he's touching he's tasting. He's like, "I know there's crab in there somewhere. I just have to find the hatch to open it …", and there goes the nose.'

I turn my attention to the little crowd with their faces pressed against the glass. Not one of them looks at all tearful. It's a chance, I realise, to witness the wonder of nature at work without fretting about the fate of a toy character. And what a wonder Ink proves to be. He's a hungry laddie!

I should say, I haven't just come here to gawp at an octopus enjoying his lunch. I'm here on account of Professor Brian Cox. I met him recently and he told me stuff about these creatures that impressed the bejesus out of me. They have nine brains and three hearts, he said. Like ours, one brain is in the head. It controls the nervous system. Then there's another brain to each arm. And the three hearts – one pumps the blood around the system and two look after the gills. And these things, the gills, are extraordinary. They can squish water out to propel the octopus about like a jet plane. For this reason alone, I would like you to stop eating octopus. Just think: you're eating all this lovely creature's nice brains! Don't do it. Eat stupid things.

And in case anyone needs convincing, Catherine invites me to see an octopus that's much smaller than Ink but has a bigger attitude. I follow her to the lower level, and then down a further set of steps to what looks like the boiler room.

'Is this their natural habitat?' I ask, but Catherine is too busy greeting the janitor and various people at work down here. I wonder if they've volunteered to be fed to the octopus. That would be most kind.

Finally, she reaches a small room with a bank of tanks on racks. She takes me to one at the end. It isn't much bigger than the kind of goldfish aquarium you'd find in your auntie's front room. The glass looks a little tougher, perhaps, and judging by the shape lurking in the water I can understand why.

'Has she ever escaped?' I ask.

'Not this girl,' says Catherine, which makes me think the octopus might just be biding her time. 'But they're very clever so they can find any kind of weakness in the lid. That's why we keep it nice and tight, but if you're not careful they can find a spot.'

I keep a close eye on the octopus. I suspect she's keeping a close eye on me.

'They look to me like they can get through tiny spaces,' I say.

'They're den animals,' Catherine tells me. 'They love living in tight, cramped spots, so the tighter the better. And there's only one hard part of their bodies, called the beak. It's right in the centre of all those arms, so if they can fit their beak through a gap they can probably fit the rest of their body through, too.'

'Slippery creatures in every sense,' I say.

Catherine proceeds to tell me a story that makes me think of sea monsters in miniature. Here she was, she says, preparing for feeding time. The lid was off the octopus tank, she adds – which I immediately consider to be a big mistake.

'It was grabbing at me and keeping me busy,' she says with terrifying nonchalance, 'when out of the corner of my eye I see an arm reach out, snatch the bowl of food and pull it into the tank.'

Cautiously, I glance at the lid again.

'So you have to be ready for them to make an escape at all times?'

A colleague joins Catherine and she tells me that all resident octopuses at the aquarium are eventually reintroduced to the wild.

'Once they're ready to mate, we take them back to where we collected them so they're able to continue with their life.'

'How wonderful,' I say, and ask if rearing a baby octopus is a joint responsibility.

Catherine's colleague puts me in the picture with disarming frankness.

'Well, the females take care of their eggs until they're ready to hatch,' she says. 'After that they pass away.'

'Oh,' I say. 'How about the males? Or does anyone care by then?'

'They'll wander around a little bit,' says Catherine, 'usually to find as many female octopuses they can, and then generally they just get old and senile.'

I return my attention to the octopus lurking in the murk. Somehow, I don't think they're in a club of their own here when it comes to long-term expectations.

TENT CITY: A POCKET OF HUMANITY

Nobody can ignore the homeless on the West Coast of America. You see them gathered under flyovers, or wheeling their belongings along the street in carts or shopping trolleys. It's one of the first things you notice, especially when you come to the nice well-known places like San Francisco, Seattle, Los Angeles or Santa Monica. Immediately you think, What's wrong with these towns that are rejecting people from the housing system? But that isn't quite the deal, as I'm about to see for myself.

You can fall off the system quite easily and rapidly here, often because of debt. And once you're off the system, it's exceptionally difficult to get back on again. In those desperate circumstances, people often gravitate westwards because it's warmer and they stand a better chance of getting a night's sleep without also getting hypothermia. It's as simple as that. Well, here in Seattle they've got Tent Cities. And the aim is to encourage the people to look after each other.

I've come to one that's in the grounds of a church. I'm here to see a fella called Lantz, so I take myself in for a wee look and a chance to get a bigger picture. As soon as I walk through the entrance, I find myself in a cross between an orderly camp site and a refugee centre. Canvas dwellings sit alongside portaloos, picnic benches, plastic chairs and pick-ups, American flags and fences fashioned from sheets of tarpaulin.

My man Lantz, so I understand, sports an epic beard. As I make my way through the grounds, I'm hoping the brotherhood of the hairy faces will get me a couple of paces. When I see a guy approaching who looks like a mirror image of me, I can be sure I've found my guide.

'This is quite a unique affair, isn't it?' I say, as we exchange a hearty handshake.

Lantz turns to show me Tent City's office, which is made from canvas. It's open-fronted. Inside, a couple of people in orange bibs sit behind camp tables. One is processing paperwork, another filling trays of plastic cups from a jug of orange squash.

'We're open twenty-four seven,' he explains. 'A set of five people run the camp in turn. They take six-hour shifts and then we change over.'

'So they're volunteers?'

'Well, there's no staff here,' says Lantz, whose firm handshake is reinforced by the focus of his attention on me. Just looking into his eyes, behind that wild and silvery facial hair, I see a learned, eloquent man. 'The camp runs itself,' he tells me. 'It's all self-managed, and everybody who stays has to work at least three shifts.'

I check out the guys in the orange bibs. None of them look like they're wearing them under duress.

'What kind of work is involved?' I ask.

'We call it security but it's basically chores,' Lantz says. 'You know, emptying the garbage, wiping tables down. We run a clean and sober camp, too,' he adds, and holds my gaze. 'We don't care if you're drinking or drugging, but you're not doing it in camp. If you're here then you're sober, because otherwise that causes fights. We've got oodles of rules, but it's a democracy. So if a rule is judged to be dumb, it gets voted out.'

I'm impressed by the system in place here. Everyone contributes and has an equal say.

'But the purpose of this place,' I press on, 'is to get people back into society, right?'

'The main thing is to get them out of the bushes and into someplace safe,' he tells me, which comes as quite a reality check. 'Sleeping in the bushes isn't sleeping. You can't sleep with one eye open.'

Tent City is busy, but it's also very peaceful. People are going about their business, but everyone is here with a shared objective: to feel protected.

As Lantz is resident here, and clearly well experienced in taking his turn with the orange vest, he invites me to look around and chat with some of the residents. It really does feel very homely here, but I'm mindful that these are people who might well have painful pasts. As it turns out, however, the first lady I stop and chat to is very happy to share her story. She's busy sweeping out her tent when I approach.

'I was laid off in December of 2013,' she says. Her neat and tidy canvas dwelling is wired up with an electric light and a lampshade fashioned from a brown paper bag. She's middle-aged, dressed elegantly, and brimming with fortitude and courage. 'It was the hardest thing because I used up my funds, my daughter was graduating and I had medical bills. I was basically sleeping out of my car, which is kind of scary for a woman. A man could probably get by,' she suggests, 'but I wasn't enjoying it. Then I was told about Tent City, and I came here.'

We chat happily for a bit, but I'm aware that I'm keeping her from her housework, and eventually say my goodbyes. A little further on, with her story on my mind still, a man in a winter hat with earmuffs puts my thoughts into words for me.

'So many people have a misconception of the homeless. You know, like everyone has to be on drugs, everyone has to be freshly out of prison.' He

A
LIZARD
OASIS

ADM 5¢
DROP
IN
BUCKET

I tell Lantz that he should be very proud of what they've achieved here. He's not here to seek praise, however, and I respect his reasons.

As I leave Tent City, I feel remarkably buoyant. I no longer see the tents first but the people, and the examples each and every one of them should be to us all. This shouldn't detract from the fact that it's terrifying how quickly you can fall into that black hole of homelessness. And getting back on your feet must feel unbelievably hard. You're nobody. You don't have an address. You don't exist. That's a rotten position to find yourself in, and yet here are people in just that situation working hard at coming together to make life good again.

You know sometimes when you find that something's going exactly according to your dreams, your heart sings a wee song to you? You find a model for society that could really exist, given half a chance, and that 'tra-la-la-la-la-la' strikes up from your chest. Well, I think that I experienced it back there; human beings in the face of adversity at their very best, at their most trusting, loyal and hard-working. I saw people doing something absolutely right for the very best of reasons. It's remarkable, and I'm deeply moved by it. In a sense it shifts your centre of gravity and silences you. That's a lovely, lovely thing, and I wish them all the very best. I'm sure you do yourself.

TWO

SEATTLE TO EL PASO

'Billy, where are we heading next?' I hear you cry. Well, let me put you in the picture. Firstly, we're off on a West Coast adventure aboard the *Coast Starlight* – an earthbound magic carpet chasing sunrises and sunsets. So take your seats as we barrel south with, through the window to our right, a view of the Pacific Ocean.

Along the way we'll stop at Portland, Oregon, a city on several levels, and in California I plan to show you one man's masterful folly as well as a wonder of the natural world that celebrates burps and blowing off. Finally, it's onwards to LA's art deco train station, where aspiring actors and actresses once arrived in search of Hollywood fame and fortune.

From there, with barely a chance to grab a coffee, we'll climb on board the *Sunset Limited*. We'll be riding the oldest train route in America – and she's going to take us east across the sun-baked splendour of the Arizona Desert. We'll relive the days when the state was host to missile silos and the end of the world loomed large, and then play out our Wild West dreams en route to our final destination on this stage of our journey: El Paso, Texas.

Portland

6

7

California

Arizona

8

9

Texas

6

PORTLAND

I leave Seattle to the rain, not that the residents mind one bit, and settle into my compartment for the second stage of this railroad round trip. What I've always loved about America is that sense of vastness. At first sight, the landscape can look as if it's all out there for the taking.

A vivid sense of hope and optimism comes with that, and it's served up in spades on board the *Coast Starlight*. As the last of Washington State rushes by my window, I look out across open plains, arable land, winding river courses, dense forest and distant ranges, but I also get to see the sky. On board Amtrak trains like this one, they've kindly coupled up carriages with transparent panels overhead. It transforms a very pleasant journey into an opportunity to wonder at both the earth and the heavens above.

I'm mindful of another Scotsman as the scenery sweeps by. John Muir, a son of Dunbar, became known as the father of American national parks. He was a staunch advocate of the US wilderness and did great things in the field of preservation. You should read about the man if you get the chance. The guy was an evangelist for the natural world. He used to clamber up rocks in order

'I've never heard of that in my life,' I say.

'You've got to do a little research,' he reasons, as we venture between the rows of plants. 'It'll open a whole new world to you.'

I push an overhanging frond from my path. It's hot inside this plastic housing, and deeply pungent.

'Is it safe to inhale in here?' I ask.

Tom assures me that I'll be fine. He wants to show me his 'go to' weed of choice. As he pokes about between the rows, I'm reminded of my own experience with weed. While I'm happy that I've left those years behind me, I do have an achingly fond memory that involved getting preposterously stoned with my former band mate, Gerry Rafferty, and merely from having dropped that name I feel duty-bound to share the memory with you.

Some of the details are hazy, for obvious reasons, but we were in Scotland at the time, in Thurso or was it Wick? Either way, we'd played a gig and had sorted our accommodation for the night. It was pretty much just someone's floor, which was how we toured in those days. Back then, I could tell you the difference between an Axminster and a Wilton carpet by the taste. There was nothing glamorous about it, but great friendships were forged by just spending time cooped up together in those circumstances.

So, Gerry and I had been sitting downstairs with our host, smoking a little bandyhoot as we called it, and just shooting the breeze, when the guy decided to call it a night. It wasn't until after he turned in, however, that we realised he'd used the last of the cigarette papers to roll a joint. Now, we'd all been drinking. It's fair to say we were shit-faced, in fact, but of course that's when the best ideas take shape. I said to Gerry, 'I'm sure I've seen a movie set in a prison where the inmates skinned up using pages from the Bible. Let's have a go at that!' The next challenge, of course, was finding a copy of the Good Book. No doubt we could've improvised, but just then nothing else would do.

Shortly after this brainwave, I knocked on the guy's bedroom door and found him reading a book in bed. It was one of those plane spotters' manuals. They're odd-shaped books: really tall with silhouettes of MiGs and Hawker Hunters.

No good for rolling up a reefer, obviously, so I said: 'Excuse me, would you have a Bible by any chance?' He says 'Aye, Billy,' and points me towards his bookshelf. When I told him why I was after it he didn't bat an eyelid. Instead, for reasons known only to him, he asked if I had any particular part of the Bible in mind. I said simply, 'Oh, Genesis will do fine,' and ripped out a couple of tissue-thin pages from near the front.

A few minutes later Gerry and I were downstairs, reading and smoking as we passed the joint between us. It wasn't as easy as you might imagine. Try reciting a verse from the Old Testament when you're stoned, where everyone *begets* and *begat* one another like crazy, and see if you can keep a straight face. I remember some big *begetting* going on between Joshua, Isaac and Ishmael, and laughing until I ached. That just wouldn't happen at any other time, and though I'm very happy that my drinking and smoking days are behind me, I still raise a smile when I think of my old friend, God rest his soul, and those foolish but priceless moments.

'Here it is!' declares Tom, which brings me back to my senses, smack in the heart of a weed farm. I blink in the sunshine, muted by the roof of the polytunnel, and find my host fondling more foliage. 'This keeps me going all day,' he tells me, which is weird because in my experience it just encourages you to sit on the sofa with biscuit crumbs all down your front. Still, Tom speaks with such sincerity that I don't question him. 'It just makes me want to work and work really hard and it takes away the pain. But you don't want to smoke too much,' he cautions. 'That wouldn't be good.'

'Why not?' I ask.

'Well, it's going to get you a little anxious. And we're not looking for that. There's enough anxiety in regular life.'

'That's what always happened to me,' I confess. 'It's the reason I stopped. It made me paranoid.'

Tom tells me it isn't such an issue when cannabis is grown organically.

'Mixing in the chemicals can give you that uptight feeling,' he explains. 'But when grown naturally like this we can focus on just really good flavour and taste.'

There's no doubt in my mind that Tom takes his subject seriously. I could be standing in a vineyard right now, listening to a master of his art talk about a grape crop destined to become a vintage wine.

'You're quite the cannabis connoisseur,' I say.

Tom acknowledges the compliment with a small nod.

'We value our patients.'

I can't ignore his choice of terminology.

'So who are they?' I ask, busting to call them 'customers'.

Tom knows just what's on my mind. I can tell by that glint in his eye before he puts me in the picture.

'Mostly the fifty- to eighty-year-olds,' he says.

'Really?'

Tom shrugs like I can take it or leave it, but I recognise an honest man when I see one.

'They're baby boomers,' he explains. 'They smoked a little bit at college and it made them feel good. Now they're retired and they want to smoke again.'

'For health reasons only?'

'Right now I'm a medicinal grower,' he says, before shooting me a look and finally relenting: 'OK, I'm hoping to segue into entertainment soon.'

I like Tom's way with words enormously. He's jolly good company, and the more I look around, the more impressed I am by his venture. When he takes me through the financial aspect, the scale of his ambitions doesn't surprise me one bit. The fact is that legalised marijuana is now the fastest-growing industry in the USA.

'The government has collected over two hundred million dollars in taxes over the last sixteen months,' he tells me, which I find astonishing. 'And that's in Washington and Colorado alone.'

With this in mind, I can understand why Tom is so dedicated to building a reputation here, along with a brand. As well as his crop, you can buy farm-themed books and mosaic artwork featuring the man himself – fashioned entirely from roach paper – but he perhaps saves the best until the end of my visit.

'This is for guests,' he says, and invites me to step inside another polytunnel. As well as more plants, this one features a clearing with a carpet, a double bed, an uplight and a sofa. 'Welcome to the grotto!'

It's an extraordinary little setup, and I can see this business opportunity being a big success. Finally, Tom invites me to sample some home-grown product. Not the cannabis, but a slice of watermelon fresh from the farm.

'You're good at what you do,' I say, and take another bite from what is the best watermelon I've ever had.

'The flavours and tastes you're getting there are what I try to achieve with my cannabis,' says Tom, and I believe him. I also doubt that he'll stop with a winning crop. The guy is a cannabis evangelist and also an explorer. He'll go on investigating how to extract the benefits from what he considers to be a holistic elixir – and who am I to deter him?

If you're ever passing through from Seattle down to Portland, I recommend you drop in on this lovely, welcoming man. What I like best about Tom is that he's brimming with optimism and totally believable. You couldn't make him up. He's one of those enthusiasts who's turned his back on the dark side of drugs and focuses solely on the properties of cannabis that people find beneficial. He sells his product well, I thought. And it's a good product, by all accounts. I hope it keeps a lot of people from boozing, and there's certainly plenty of evidence that it helps ease the pain and suffering of diseases like glaucoma. Then there are the cancer patients who use the drug to ease the side effects associated with chemotherapy. How can that be a bad thing, eh?

I've always been in favour of marijuana becoming legal, above all to keep the gangsters out of the market. Tom is the kind of man you could trust to do business fairly and with the best of intentions. I could have happily stayed on his farm for hours and hours, maybe even spent the night in that wee grotto amid all the plants. I was dying to, in fact, because it looked like pure joy, but as ever I had a train to catch. Despite not being able to chalk off waking up on a hash farm from my bucket list, I'm still so glad I met Tom Lauerman, someone who embodies pure happiness. As a kind soul doing good things, I wish him every success. He's the nicest cannabis producer you could ever wish to meet.

AS ABOVE, SO BELOW: THE SHANGHAI TUNNELS

Riding the *Coast Starlight* is a neat, sleek way to see how the landscape changes as we make our way to Portland. Even as clouds begin to thicken overhead, dulling the light upon the land, I still find myself marvelling at the sheer scale and natural diversity that this country has to offer.

Most of all, travelling by train allows me to truly appreciate America's vast empty spaces. You can do it by road, of course, but if you're behind the wheel or grasping the handlebars of your motorbike then you really need to concentrate on the way ahead. From my seat in this carriage, by contrast,

I can just tune out and daydream as we cross prairie, scrubland and meadow, then plunge through evergreen forests. It just suits me, you know? The scenery changes constantly and I'm comfortable with that. It probably means I'm losing my ability to concentrate, but sometimes landmarks seize my attention that nobody could ignore. As we close in on our next destination, from the far horizon two snow-crested mountains preside over the terrain. These are Mount Rainier and Mount Saint Helens. If you were to take a picture postcard of Portland, they'd be hovering in the background like two proud parents.

Once upon a time, Portland was a central player in the logging industry. Not only were there trees in abundance, but the city's location where the Willamette and Columbia rivers join quickly transformed it into a transport hub. In the mid-nineteenth century, Portland underwent such a period of expansion that it picked up the nickname Stumptown. This was down to the number of trees that were felled to make way for new roads. But its nickname doesn't exactly sell what is a strikingly welcoming place. Nor does it reflect its recent popularity as a home for young Americans in search of a more laid-back way of life.

Leaving the station exit, I choose to avoid the hipster hangouts. They may well be plentiful in this liberal metropolis, but instead I head for a less well documented, less desirable area: skid row. Actually, I take myself *underneath* skid row and into a network of tunnels. These are hidden below the streets near the waterfront and extend all the way downtown. Now, there are several schools of thought about the purpose of this old subterranean warren. Some argue that it was simply a means of getting across town when the streets were muddy and largely impassable. Others say it was used to transport goods from the docks to the many basements under the hotels and bars, thereby avoiding the traffic above ground. But I'm particularly drawn to a more sinister claim: namely, that the tunnels were a means for press gangs to snatch unsuspecting individuals, then sell them on to sea captains. From there, these poor souls could look forward to nothing better than a life of hard labour at sea.

The practice was known as 'shanghaiing', and these catacombs are called the Shanghai Tunnels. They're dark and dingy, as you might expect: a labyrinth of claustrophobic brick passageways, columns and secret stairways. Now, in the golden age of the waterways, Portland earned a reputation for being a dangerous place. With a hive of saloon bars and brothels to cater for the ranchers, sailors and stevedores who gathered here, the waterfront in particular was notorious for fights and robberies. Even if you had no intention of getting into trouble, the threat from below ground was ever present. Poking about in the gloom, well aware that countless trapdoors once linked this shadowy network to the world above, I find my imagination running away with me. For if men weren't snatched from the streets by thugs, or slipped a knockout drug and dragged down the steps with a one-way ticket to the high seas, they could literally find themselves dropping through the floor. Some poor guy could be in a bar downtown, enjoying a bevvy and chatting up a few women. He sits back on his stool and all of a sudden the ground appears to give way. Boom! The next thing he knows, it's goodbye Mum and Dad, hello sailor!

What's really striking is this practice continued until remarkably recently. There was a letter in the newspaper here, in 1939, from one Mr Clarke of Washington. While holidaying in Portland, he claimed to have fallen victim to kidnappers. His ordeal had begun following a lovely riverboat cruise. He'd enjoyed a drink, as was his right, and was looking forward to dancing the night away on deck. Now, according to our man, at one point the ship's captain had approached him and said, 'Would you like to go and have a look at my square rig?' That's not a double entendre. It's a type of sail you see on tall ships. Being a courteous guy, no doubt, with an interest in all things maritime, Mr Clarke accepted the captain's invitation. So, the riverboat set a course for this huge vessel. Before boarding the ship, Clarke claimed, he was asked to sign a safety certificate. The benefit of hindsight might've alerted him to the fact that he had just effectively signed his life away. And indeed, rather than enjoying a guided tour of an impressive ocean-going ship, he found himself heading out to sea – not just for a demonstration run, but for a gruelling 120-day voyage to France via South America. The poor guy allegedly had to man the decks alongside the seafarers, and was even obliged to pay on reaching port in order to secure his release.

Now Mr Clarke's tale is notable in Portland's press-gang history for taking place just under seventy years ago. But the most famous Shanghai snatcher operated in the nineteenth century and went by the name of Bunko Kelly. It's said that he once seized and sold twenty men to a sea captain, but it isn't the number that makes this story so remarkable so much as the fact that all the men turned out to be dead. At the time, shanghaiing could earn you fifty bucks per head. Given the effort in snatching victims – especially with the risk of them fighting back – it was probably a fair price, and so Bunko couldn't believe his luck when he discovered a big group of guys sprawled out in a cellar. They'd been drinking embalming fluid, having mistaken it for alcohol, and were all close to death.

The quick-thinking Bunko wrapped each groaning victim in blankets and transported them through the tunnels to the ship, where the captain awaited. It wasn't unusual for captured men to show up dazed or drugged, and Bunko received payment in full before vanishing into the shadows. As for the captain, can you imagine his face when he opened the hatch next morning, on the high seas? There he would've stood, the daylight behind him, keen to rouse his new additions to the crew, only to find he had bought twenty already cooling corpses. Eventually Kelly was caught by the police, charged with murder and sent to prison for fifteen years, but not before he had scammed another naval captain by wrapping a carved wooden effigy in a blanket and passing it off as a live man. Either Bunko was a very convincing con artist or the sea captains in those days needed their eyes testing.

Back in the natural light, on emerging from the Shanghai Tunnels I'm struck by the sudden transformation from past to present. Here on skid row I see people living out their lives on the streets, some clearly with nowhere else to go, and once again this country's growing homelessness crisis hits me.

It reminds me of the time I visited Portland once before. I was with my daughter, who isn't just my pal but also my roadie. We were unaccustomed to the city and wandered into a rather less salubrious area much like this one. A homeless guy on a walking frame hobbled up to us. I gave him a dollar and he said: 'Where are you guys going?', then carried on shuffling along right beside us. 'Are you looking for a restaurant?' he pressed on. 'Let me tell you about a great place to eat. I can promise you now, you'll never taste food like it.' So I did that thing where you thank the fellow, say '*Cheerio!*', and then we hurried across the road to get away. Only, he followed, the ferrules of his walking frame clanking with every step, and caught up! 'You're going the wrong way!' he insisted. 'You want the place back there!' Now, I felt bad for thinking this at the time and it haunted me, but I didn't feel inclined to take culinary advice from a homeless person. So when we spied a restaurant that looked decent, my daughter and I dived in. 'Don't go there!' he yelled. 'The food's rotten!' By this point I'd stopped smiling and being polite. I just wanted to get away, and he knew it. 'I hope you get the shits!' he raged, and that was that.

As it turned out, the food was fine, but the encounter left a bad taste in my mouth. I'm not quite sure how I should've handled it, but looking back I think the guy was being genuine and I had just dismissed him in my mind as a pest. In a way, that sense of uneasiness I experienced comes back to me as I make my way through the quarter. I think it comes down to the fact that Portland is clearly a very popular place to live. It's affluent, easy-going and picture-perfect in many respects. Then you find pockets like this, but unlike Tent City there's an atmosphere here, as if the residents just don't know how to handle the homeless, and the homeless don't know how to deal with the residents. That makes me feel uncomfortable, because I want to see everyone getting along. But I also want to be part of the solution, not the problem, which is why I hope I learned something valuable from that guy who had just wanted me to engage with him.

I wonder what this means. Something tells me it involves a lot more than a gift for getting a good night's sleep in a ditch.

'How do you become a good one?'

Even before Whitey answers me, I'm pretty sure that if anyone knows, it's him.

'You have to love being a train rider,' he begins, as if it really is as simple as that. Then he draws breath and I just know I'm going to learn something that will stay with me. 'I've always been one of the running kind,' he continues. 'Leaving was always on my mind. Home was never home to me at any time.'

This reminds me of a saying by the protest singer Phil Ochs, and I share it with Whitey in the hope that it'll chime with him.

'"There's no problem so big you can't run away from it."'

Once again, much to my delight, Whitey's expression comes alive.

'Oh, Phil was a great one,' he says, then his voice trails away. 'He's dead now, though.'

'Everyone I know is dead,' I reply.

'I was just about to say that.'

I warn him that he'd better watch out, now he's met me, and we both laugh again. I am enormously drawn to this man. Not just because he's lived a life I hold in high esteem. He's simply a lovely old boy with a spark that still burns brightly. When he plays me another tune, I sit back and wonder whether he might live for ever. To my ears, his music sounds timeless.

'Can I ask when you first became a hobo?' I say when he has finished.

In Guitar Whitey's company, that word doesn't feel at all disparaging. It's more like a badge of honour. The way he responds, it's clearly one he wears with pride.

'I was thirteen years old.'

'Is that all?'

In my short time with him, almost everything he's told me leaves me both surprised and delighted. I ask what led him into a life riding the railroads.

'It wasn't because my parents were poor or because the Depression was on,' he's quick to say. 'It's just every time you saw a train in those days there'd be anything from one to two hundred hobos on board.'

'Really?'

Again, Whitey leaves me astonished.

'I just thought, That's what I want to do, and so I fooled around so I could finally do it.'

'Where did you go for your first ride?'

'Seattle to Portland,' he says, which makes me feel like I've recently followed in his tracks. 'It was two hundred miles on a fast merchandised train called *Hotshot*. I spent a little bit of time in Portland and came back the next night. That was my first ride.'

'What did your father think of that?'

'I didn't tell him. I lied about it. I told him I went to my friend's house and my friend told his parents he went to my house.'

'So you went on that first trip together?'

Whitey nods, beaming.

'Yeah, my friend and me.'

'That's *lovely*,' I say, and I have no doubt that he can remember every moment, from the fear and elation that must've accompanied the moment they stole on board to the fun and excitement of a grand adventure at such a tender age.

'I couldn't get enough of it,' he adds. 'And finally I became a fruit tramp. Are you familiar with that term?'

I imagine the look on my face confirms a no. 'But it sounds wonderful,' I point out.

Whitey is leaning on the edge of his guitar now, as if against a bar.

'In the late days of the Depression,' he begins, 'you would go out and pick cherries, pick apples, pick potatoes and make from one dollar to two dollars a day. It was dandy. That was living, all right. For two dollars a day you could buy all the groceries you were able to carry in two arms. I travelled all around

I've always been one of the running kind,' he continues. 'Leaving was always on my mind. Home was never home to me at any time.'

Oregon, Washington, California, Idaho and parts of Montana. That was the territory.'

'And you'd travel by rail?'

'Yep,' he says. 'Between jobs we'd ride the free trains.'

These days, I'm well aware, the practice would be known as fare dodging. It strikes me as being so different back then. An age of innocence, perhaps, now lost for ever. And all the more reason, I realise, why the stories people like Guitar Whitey can tell serve as an oral history of a bygone age.

'Was there money to be made from being a fruit hobo?' I ask.

'I'd pick the apples up in Washington and come away in late October or November with fifty dollars cash money tucked away in my shoe.'

This strikes me as being a considerable sum in those days, but I soon learn that Whitey earned the money to fulfil responsibilities back home.

'I'd send it all back to my mother,' he tells me. 'That would be enough to take her through the whole winter. Basically, my sisters and my mother would live on what I made as a fruit tramp.'

Countless questions come to mind. Having always been interested in the lifestyle Guitar Whitey lived and breathed, I want to hear what it was really like.

'Did you ever live in a hobo jungle?'

'Yeah, I lived in one,' he confirms.

I hope he's impressed that I'm familiar with the term. In the days when drifters moved around the railroads in large numbers, they'd often gather in gorges or clearings. They came together for warmth – there'd be a nice fire burning – companionship or rest. I think about Seattle's Tent City as Whitey shares his experience. The similarities are striking.

'They called it the jungle because often it was in woodland. It meant you could hide out a while and feel safe. Outside those places, you're just standing there for God and everybody to see you, and that just brings the bulls down.'

Whitey tells me that 'bull' is hobo slang for a railroad operative – and it doesn't paint a picture of some kindly ticket inspector. Indeed, I can imagine that when a drifter rocked up in a strange town, he didn't always meet with a hearty welcome. Embracing the wanderer within, I think, must have required a streetwise sensibility.

'Why did the police dislike hobos so much?' I ask. 'In the films I've seen or anything I've read about, they were very cruel. They used to beat them, right?'

Guitar Whitey sits upright as he nods.

'Oh, the cops would beat the brains out of them,' he says plainly. 'Sometimes in Texas they'd shoot them.'

'Really?'

I'm not so much surprised, this time, as genuinely shocked.

'Shoot them right off the trains,' adds Whitey, a man who has clearly earned his spurs. 'So you'd hide in the weeds, or a hobo jungle, until a train comes. Then you'd run for it. You'd pick your car, hop on and ride …' He grins broadly, as if he knows there's no need to go any further. 'Ain't that something? What a life!'

I find myself relishing the moment with him. It sounds like a hellishly dangerous existence, but unquestionably exciting.

'When did it all come to an end for you?' I ask.

He considers my question, patting the side of his guitar. When he answers, there's a sombre note in his voice.

'The year 2000 was the last time I hopped a freight train,' he begins, and I work out that would've put him in his eighties. 'I rode with a convict who I didn't know was a convict. He had just killed some people and I didn't know that. Still, he was just as nice to me as if he had been my son. He took good care of me on that ride, and this is the guy who killed all these people.'

I'm stunned into silence for a second. Then, somewhere in the back of my mind, I realise that the story sounds faintly familiar.

'Was he killing people on the hobo runs?' I ask, for I vaguely remember hearing about it in the news around that time.

'He had these demons that would attack him,' Whitey explains, 'and when they came he had to kill somebody. That was the moment I decided to stop. It made me realise how close I came to having my head smashed in.'

When I think of all the stories of my own that I can tell my grandchildren, absolutely nothing compares to this. I also have no doubt that Whitey could continue spinning them for hours and I would happily listen. But we're approaching another stop now and this is where my new friend must get off. I'm sorry we have to finish this conversation, but I know it'll stay with me for the rest of my days.

Being in Guitar Whitey's company for a short while was a real privilege, not least because as we said our goodbyes he told me that he sensed I understood him. I hope I did. As my train pushes on south for the state line, and with my banjo picking up my voice, I hope I carry with me just a drop of Whitey's eternally free spirit.

was awarded this great honour for canoeing across San Francisco Bay in a craft made from cigar boxes. He seems like my kind of guy.

Poking around the back, I find his workshop. It looks like he spent a great deal of time here, which is no surprise. The man must've been a creative livewire. Then there's the outdoor cooking facility, with rusting pots and pans dotted about the landscape. I'm sorry to hear that some of the neighbours hate this place. They want it pulled down, by all accounts. I would fight them every inch of the way. In fact, during my visit a lady drove by who must have been from one of the houses behind. She pulls up, winds down her window and says haughtily, 'We live above it.' She might be right in the geographical sense. In every other way, Nitt Witt Ridge towers above everything else in this neighbourhood. In fact, the next time the residents get themselves into a stew because the guttering isn't perfectly aligned with the horizon, they should remind themselves that Arthur Beal was here first. The fact that the place is now designated a California Historical Landmark assures me that its existence is safe for some time.

Mind you, when I follow the stairwell that takes me to the roof, I realise that the owner might've purposely set out to ruffle gentrified feathers. For this is where I find the seat on which Arthur liked to settle and then harangue passers-by. It's basically an old toilet, bolted onto one corner like a castle battlement, and I should imagine that when he went on to throw stones some people might well have got on to the local authorities. I try out the porcelain

throne for size and can't resist unleashing my inner curmudgeon. How wonderful! Every home should have one of these. Now go on, *bugger off*!

There's another residence of note around here. Just a few miles away stands Hearst Castle. Designed for that controversial newspaper owner Randolph Hearst, it's better known than Nitt Witt Ridge, but the two buildings might well have more in common than meets the eye. For it's said that Arthur once worked up at the estate, taking away discarded bits and bobs that he then put to good use. Isn't that great? So, while Hearst built his empire, Beal used its rubbish to lay the foundations for his own little world.

In 1989, like so many people coming into their prime, Arthur Beal was carted off to an old folks' home against his will. Unsurprisingly, he wasn't content to sit quietly in a comfy chair waiting to sip his dinner through a straw. Instead, he escaped and hitch-hiked all the way back to Nitt Witt Ridge. And who could blame him for being so single-minded, having built a house that expressed his own character to a T? Not me. What's more, having presumably stocked up on stones he could throw at anyone who might try to take him away again, Arthur stayed put until his death in 1992 at the ripe old age of ninety-six. His ashes are scattered around a favourite tree nearby, but I think his spirit lives on in the marvellous legacy he left behind.

In my view, Arthur's house is folk art at its finest. It's a living, breathing, fully functional creation of a unique mind. I'll be honest, before I laid eyes on the place I had assumed that the man was a nutter. As I leave, I make a note to myself not to be so quick to draw conclusions in future. Yes, the guy liked to perch on a toilet on the roof and shout at people he didn't like, but who am I to judge him for that? Like or loathe what he built over half a lifetime, Nitt Witt Ridge oozes character, and we seem to be living in an age when that's frowned upon. If you're famous and show a bit of spirit, the media leap upon it, chase you day and night, and generally make your life a misery. Eccentricity should be something we celebrate, so I'm pleased that Arthur's work has been recognised for its significance.

The house is in a run-down state right now, but the new owners do tours for the public and are in the process of restoring it to its former glory. I'd love to see that and they have my full support. I look at all those TV house-buying shows that encourage you to pop an apple pie in the oven before viewings so as to influence potential buyers and it just seems so redundant when I look at a place like this. If you want to see a two-fingered salute to town planning that has nothing to do with greed or ostentation and everything to do with bloody-minded creativity, come and visit Nitt Witt Ridge. You won't be disappointed.

MY BIG FAT LOVE-IN: THE ELEPHANT SEALS OF SAN SIMEON

Before we rejoin the *Coast Starlight* and journey down to Los Angeles, I want to see a sight that I'm told will take my breath away. It's only a short hop from Nitt Witt Ridge and it offers a chance to enjoy the splendour of the Pacific coastline. You can't beat the breakers that form as the waves roll in, or the deep-blue tones of the water. Surfers are drawn to spots along this stretch between the bluffs, so poised and muscular as they float and bob on the swells. Unfortunately, the same can't be said of the group I've come to visit, who are flopped across the shore a little further up the coast. Even before I've laid eyes on these guys, the sound of belching and farting from beyond the sand dunes hardly screams *Baywatch* to me.

This is San Simeon, California. It's a little town that comprises a couple of hundred houses. The beach here is overrun by a species that rolls in looking for some sun on their backs, a spot of violence … and sex.

I'm not talking about the kind of holidaymakers you might find in certain resorts all around the world. These are elephant seals. When I finally lay eyes on them, carpeting the sand like vastly overgrown sardines, it looks like little more than a love-handles festival.

Now, the whole point of this gathering is to procreate. The males aim to get a harem together and they fight each other to keep the gene pool high. Some of the more combative boys have been known to waddle up to the car park and pick a fight with an innocent vehicle. I wouldn't fancy that. One minute you're eating your sandwiches, admiring the ocean horizon, the next thing some blubbery psycho is all over your bonnet claiming that you're looking at him funny.

Even if they can fight off the competition, only about a third of the males get to have sex. The rest are doomed to wander the oceans of the world shagless for the rest of their lives. All in all, it's a deeply unfair affair. I'd like to say it's about survival of the fittest, but honestly I don't see much sign of activity amongst this flatulent bunch. There's not even a hint of any love action. Maybe I arrived just as they all finished, I think to myself. None of them are smoking a post-coital cigarette, but that's the vibe I encounter.

There are literally hundreds of them here, crammed side by side and even on top of each other. I keep a respectful distance, mindful that most are a hefty size, but they're too busy flopping about and dozing to notice me. Still, I'm close enough to recognise that these animals are obese, and the noise they make is pure comedy. What's great is that they've been coming here for centuries and yet evolution appears to have given up on them. And do they seem to care? Not one bit. Honestly, they don't give a shit. And I'll tell you how that leaves me feeling – *jealous*. Pure and simple. As an elephant seal, I could be swimming around with my mates one day and one of us might suggest we hit the beach to see if we can get laid. So I'd waddle onto the shore with my posse, engage in a mindless fist-fight, then wedge myself between the chicks and hope I strike lucky. What a life, eh? Personally, I'm all for it. Especially the belching and farting.

I'm close enough to recognise that these animals are obese, and the noise they make is pure comedy.

THE RESTORATION OF AN ANGEL: APPROACHING UNION STATION

I reflect on the injustice of life as I rejoin the *Coast Starlight* for the final stretch of her journey down to Los Angeles. As tempted as I might be to just let it all hang out, I'm aware that I'm amongst fare-paying passengers and turn my attention towards our destination. Yet again the terrain shifts as we hurtle onwards. The valleys here are deeply fertile, and we pass acres of carefully planted crops. It really does feel like the basket of the world, as if humans have harnessed nature here so as to put food on the table. I think of the fruit hobos and the migrant workers once again, and the stories of hardship through history that underpin this agricultural bed. And then slowly but surely the landscape begins to shift again. Buildings and roads become more numerous, then take over completely in a network of lights as we approach the City of Angels.

Union Station is a fine example of railway restoration. It's a hugely important hub for three major lines, including the *Coast Starlight* Amtrak route from Seattle, and a unique combination of art deco and Spanish colonial style. Located in the downtown area, which isn't known for its glamour, the station shines out like a diamond. Built in the 1930s, as nearby Hollywood basked in its golden age, this is where actors and actresses arrived with a suitcase full of dreams and ambition. It was an age of high hopes and charming innocence, both of which would come to an end as World War Two cast its shadow over the land. That moment in time is easily forgotten, what with the dark days that followed, and yet there's something very special about it that we could all do with remembering.

Thanks to the efforts of those behind the restoration project, arriving at Union Station seems like a return to that lost age. Just stepping off the train into this marble and terracotta temple to travel, it's easy to feel as if you've arrived in more ways than one. Whether you're an aspiring actor or an old soul with an appreciation of the past, every pillar and tile feels as if it's been painted or polished purely for your benefit. It's a wonderful place to finish up at after a long journey and a very pleasant staging post if you're here to begin another. For this is the end of the line for the *Coast Starlight* and the point of departure for our next adventure. This time, we're bound for New Orleans on board … the *Sunset Limited*.

I can barely process how that must feel, facing the big screen wondering if Doomsday is upon you.

'It must've been a huge relief when the missiles changed their course,' I say.

Yvonne nods, then tells me it wasn't as scary as the geese.

'A flock would show up on the radar, in the days when a blip could've been a bunch of birds in formation or something much, much worse. All of a sudden everyone in mission control is up on their feet once again.'

'It must've been very stressful,' I say.

'Solar flares could also trigger a warning,' she goes on. 'We just had to wait until absolutely the last second to confirm that it wasn't really a launch. Fortunately, we were able to stand down every single time.'

Yvonne seems genuinely reassuring, but it sounds like a horribly high-stakes game to be playing. I have to confess that when the Cold War was at its frostiest, I never lived in fear. I did the CND marches, but mostly to get women, which pretty much governed every decision in my life back then. The only time that didn't figure was when I took up playing the banjo. From bitter experience, I can tell you now that nobody shags the banjo player. It's one of those lines you never hear: 'Oh yeah, she's sleeping with the banjo player.' Anyway, I remember the Cuban missile crisis of 1962, which was the closest America and Russia came to unleashing their arsenals at each other. Someone said that if negotiations failed, then the world would end at 3 p.m. that Friday. Around 3.15 that day, I remember looking up thinking Well, it's nae gonna end now. I left work at the shipyard that evening and passed a newspaper seller outside. The guys rushed to buy the paper and every single one of them turned to the back pages. Nobody gave a shit about Castro, Kennedy or Cuba. You lived for work and that was it. Had I known Yvonne at the time, of course, and the potential consequences if she suffered a bad day at the office, I would've been a lot more concerned.

'Was there ever a little part of you that just wanted to turn the key?' I ask.

'Billy, there was a big part of me wanted to do that.'

She stops there and smiles wryly.

'Go on,' I say. 'I won't tell anyone.'

'All right,' she relents after a moment. 'Between ourselves, there was a little part of me that wanted to run screaming from the room, but also a very big part of me that's pretty sure I could've done it if I had to. I mean, my family lives one hundred miles south of Washington DC. By the time I got a launch order, they'd be gone. Life as I knew it would be over. For me, that was a lot of motivation. Payback is absolutely necessary in that instance.'

I don't doubt Yvonne's word here. She speaks with utter conviction, as if it's something she's considered over a long period.

'I don't know if *I* could've done it,' I confess.

'Well, you know, I don't think everybody can,' she says, as if to console me, 'and fortunately it's not necessary. The whole reason that I came to work every day was because it wasn't *my* mission to launch the missile. We were part of a big machine that's projecting a credible threat. One that says to the former Soviet Union: "Listen, we've got the biggest, baddest missiles on the block. Even if you launch against us first, we are going to come back at you so hard that you're not going to survive it either and so you don't want to take us on." That was my job,' she finishes, with steel in her voice. 'Peace through deterrence.'

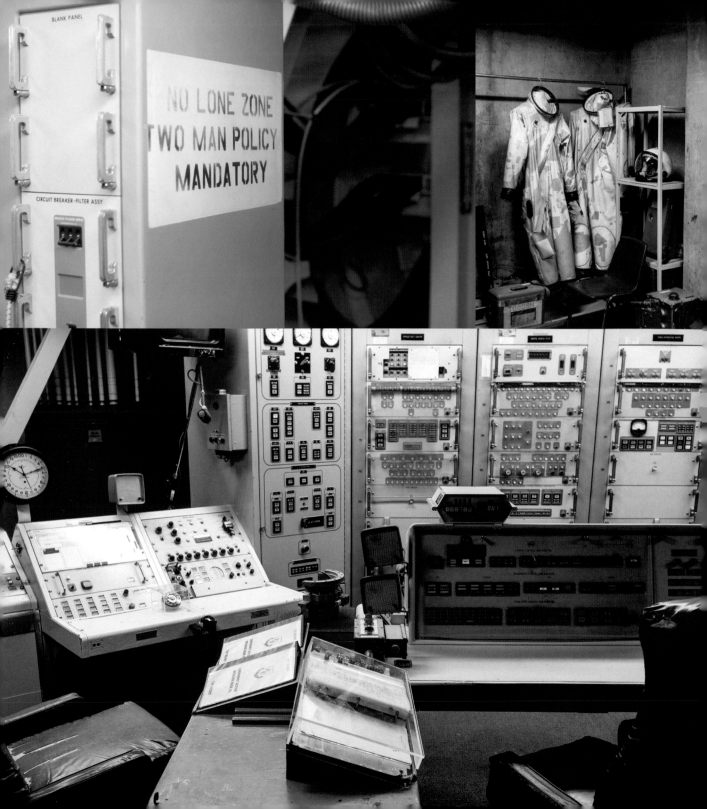

'Did you sleep OK?' I ask, because I'm interested in what impact this line of work can have on a person. I'd have been staring at the ceiling until dawn, make no mistake. With calm authority, Yvonne tells me she slept just fine.

'Better than I do now, in fact,' she adds. 'We knew who the enemy was back then. Today it's not as clear cut.'

I tell her that's just what was on my mind as I travelled here. The facility on the other side of this fence, like many others across the region, has been decommissioned as we focus our efforts on combating a very different kind of threat. Reflecting on the days when silos like this were deemed critical, I wonder if the personnel here ever found a way to let off steam.

'Did you ever have end-of-the-world parties?' I ask a little mischievously, and then Yvonne wipes the smile from my face by confirming that they happened on a regular basis.

'Actually, the very last event that we had was called a top-of-the-door party. They threw it right on top of the silo closure door that covers the launch duct. There were tables up there and we had a band. It was great!'

I look across at the military buildings. The sun beats down and sand drifts across the grounds.

'It's weird to think this is a historic site,' I say. 'It feels like it was all going on only yesterday.'

Yvonne reminds me that the nation is still vigilant.

'The United States has about four hundred intercontinental ballistic missiles,' she says. 'Russia has continental ballistic missiles still on alert. North Korea may be building them. China has them as well, so it *is* kind of yesterday but it's also very much today.'

I think about the Russians and the picture we used to paint of generals in fur-lined hats smattered with snow. Yvonne tells me she recently met her Soviet counterpart.

'He lives in Texas with his family now,' she says. 'He's a lovely man, and when he visited here we shook hands and thanked each other for not launching.'

I'm delighted by the story of this little encounter. I also tell her that as an old hippy I wish the pair had met decades before and agreed never to launch. Yvonne holds back a smile, but I register it clearly.

'I'm kind of with you on that,' she says, to finish.

I'm always astounded when I meet people like Yvonne. She had this incredibly important position. When she went to work each morning, the future of the Western world was effectively in her hands. And yet she's just so ordinary, like you and me, and I mean that in the nicest possible way. I'm pleased she was smart and sensible, and not some fuckwit yahoo with an urge to kill folk. Then again, with a job like hers, I think I expected to meet someone more sinister, like the devil with fiery horns. That's never the case, of course, as I imagine Yvonne must've recognised for herself when she met her Russian opposite. In the same way, the man who makes the landmines no doubt drops off his children at school before going to work. And he's making this nightmarish object and justifying it in his own mind by saying he's hoping to take out the bad guys. It always leaves me in a total quandary. On the one hand, I should be grateful for the protection such professionals afford me, but shouldn't I also be horrified that they're doing it in my name? I think this will puzzle me for the rest of my life.

BORDERLAND LIVES: THE TWO SIDES OF TUCSON

A good trip, in my book, should be littered with little detours. Travelling from A to B is all very well, but you risk missing out on so much. So instead of climbing back on board the *Sunset Limited* straight away, I'm off on a wee jaunt by helicopter. Having just spent time with Yvonne outside the missile base, I take one look at the military chopper and wonder if I'm about to be flown into battle. In a way, that's just what's going on down on the border. For Arizona is one of four states that neighbour Mexico. The fence that divides the two countries runs for two thousands miles and by all accounts it isn't the most effective tool against migration and drug smuggling.

This long-running situation has also led to a battle between the authorities and people who have settled on what the law considers to be the wrong side of the line.

The flight is spectacular, providing glimpses of the fencing and, especially, a bird's-eye view of rugged mountain ranges and of the extent of the military's presence in this region. Most of the missile silos are closed, but we fly over an airbase with jets of every size and description on the ground, arranged in perfect rows. It's a reminder that America is still a superpower that can call upon sophisticated technology to protect itself. Having said that, the border patrol force I'm about to meet relies on a more traditional piece of kit.

I arrive at what looks like a horse-riding school. It's a little bit more serious than that, however, as becomes evident when a woman strides across to greet me wearing khaki fatigues, military boots and a utility belt.

'How are you today, sir?' asks Bobbi, my guide to the work undertaken by the patrols.

I tell her I'm enjoying the Arizona heat. Being Scottish, it's a rare treat.

'I've never been,' she says, beaming at me politely. I'm not entirely sure she knows where Scotland is, but her manner is lovely. 'Let me show you around.'

Bobbi is a warm host who's clearly at home in this environment. She shows me the stables where the horses used to undertake patrols reside, and then moves on to the sand school. There, several brawny patrolmen in Stetsons stand talking in front of their steeds.

'Most of our horses are being trained right now, so these are the older guys.'

She leads me towards one of the horses. I shoot one of the patrolmen a funny look. At first I had thought she was talking about him.

'Is this a mustang?' I ask, in a bid to sound knowledgeable, for I do at least know that this is the name for a wild horse that's been tamed.

Bobbi steers my attention to another patrolman. He's just ambled up on a horse the size of a bus.

'This one is a mustang,' she tells me, and pats the side of the horse's neck. 'You can see in the freeze-branding here,' she adds. I take a good look at the marking. 'All mustangs have a freeze-brand identifier that is unique to that horse.'

With patrol guys who look like cowboys, and talk of mustangs and branding, this strikes me as being a far cry from the high-tech aircraft we've just flown in to get here.

'So what can you do with horses that you can't with drones and stuff?' I ask.

Bobbi leans against the stock fencing and puts me in the picture. 'There's a vital airborne element to their work in patrolling the border,' she tells me, 'but also limits to what the choppers and drones can do. We operate in a lot of mountainous and rugged terrain,' she goes on. 'They can see from above. They can tell us what is down on the ground but they can't go in. That's when the horses are vital. They're the ground assets. We use them to bring people in, seize narcotics and anything like that.'

Drug smuggling is a serious problem here, which explains the level of resources thrown into the border patrol force. The combination of horses and choppers in the sky seems like a clash of old and new. According to Bobbi, it can prove very effective.

'How about tracking?' I ask, mindful of other traditional methods of law enforcement.

Bobbi turns to her colleague on horseback for an answer. It quickly becomes apparent that the guy has first-hand experience.

'When I first joined this unit, my horse tracked down a dope haul,' he says. 'Just being a wild animal, they have better senses. They can see and hear stuff we can't, and so they'll pick it up and alert us.' He reaches down to pat his steed. 'His ears will come up, or he'll look up,' he explains. 'His head will come up and you can feel his body change when you're in the saddle. You just know there's something around there that you need to start paying attention to.'

I ask what his main function is as a patrolman. 'Is it to catch drug smugglers or illegal immigrants?'

'Both,' he says from under the brim of his hat.

'So you're busy here.'

This time, Bobbi answers. 'It's picking up again,' she says. 'Back in 2004, it wasn't unheard of to catch groups of one hundred twenty to one hundred fifty at a time.'

The number brings home just what these guys are facing. Working alongside patrols in California, New Mexico and Texas, they have a lot of difficult ground to cover here in Arizona.

'How many of you go out on patrol?' I ask.

Bobbi informs me that three or four will ride out.

'People used to be a bit more cooperative,' she adds. 'They didn't run as much.'

'You get a lot more respect on horseback,' says her colleague from the saddle. 'Even from the larger groups. They see us coming, even from a couple of ridges away, and just drop their packs, sit down and wait for us to get there. They know that they aren't going to outrun the horses.' He pats his ride once more.

'With the horses we have a higher apprehension rate.'

I want to know how they feel about the people they round up. Not the smugglers – the ordinary men, women and children who are looking for a better life north of the border.

'Do you have respect for them?' I ask.

The patrol guy considers my question.

'All of us, I think, treat them with respect and most of us respect them,' he says after a second. 'I mean, they're still breaking the law, you know? All we're doing is enforcing the law and it has nothing to do with who they are. Unfortunately, they didn't come in the right way so we have to round them up and make sure they go back. The laws are there to protect this country, not just from threats but also from diseases and all kinds of things. So, there's really not a lot of feeling in it,' he admits. 'We're just doing our job.'

I do understand and I tell him that. Even so, as the patrol prepare to head on out, I admit this is the last thing I expected to see. I had just assumed that the USA monitored its borders with high-tech surveillance equipment. There's something quite reassuring about the fact that we still rely on horses and the animals' instinct to pick up things beyond our range. We may well be living in a modern world where some guy fresh from college can pilot a drone from thousands of miles away, but there are tried and tested methods that sometimes just can't be beaten.

As I get ready to head back into town I'm well aware, as always, that I've only picked up on half the story here. The men and women who patrol this border have a difficult and often dangerous job, but I wonder what it must be like for those who feel they have no other option but to take their chances with the crossing.

Rosa Robles has lived in Tucson with her husband since the turn of the millennium. They have two sons. Both are natural born American citizens. Rosa is a measured, dignified lady, but she's in a desperate situation. With the border under pressure from an increasing number of migrants, Arizona state laws underwent a recent tightening. Having arrived on a visa that subsequently expired, Rosa discovered she faced deportation and the prospect of separation from her family.

'I feel like I'm from here,' she told my director, Mike, through an interpreter. 'This is my country. Over sixteen years I've earned the right to work here, for the opportunity to make a better life.'

Rather than be sent back to Mexico and see her family torn apart, Rosa took sanctuary in a local Presbyterian church and hasn't left the grounds for the last eighteen months. During this time, she's received huge support from the local community, including petitions and letters protesting at her planned deportation. She's quite evidently made a valuable contribution to life here, as a mother, wife, friend and neighbour.

'My children are from here,' she continues. 'They don't know Mexico. Their life, their *home*, is the United States. That's why we're fighting. I feel just like a citizen, but without the papers.'

Rosa is not alone in her plight. There are many others faced with a similar situation and no easy answers. As a visitor hoping to gain some insight, I leave feeling as if someone, somewhere, has to grasp this issue and resolve it. For an American baseball mom to feel she has no choice but to take refuge in a church is a sorry state of affairs. And so I'm pleased to report that shortly after my director visited the church, Rosa received an assurance from the authorities that she would be free to return to her home in Tucson. The threat of deportation had been lifted, and my hope is that for other people with their lives on hold, Rosa's victory will be the chink of light that might well turn to sunshine.

9

TEXAS

From my carriage window, rattling through New Mexico on our way to the Lone Star State, there can be no doubt that we're into Wild West territory. The landscape is barren and sun-baked, with canyons and wind-sculpted sandstone to fire my imagination.

It's easy to fall into daydreams about riding horseback into town, where the locals take one look at you then hurry inside for safety. By the time we pull in at El Paso, Texas, I'm surprised not to see WANTED posters with my face all over them, and a reward for my capture, dead or alive.

Instead, I find a very pleasant county seat at the foot of the Franklin Mountains. The city contains the largest urban park in the United States, making it very green, and sits alongside Ciudad Juárez in the Mexican state of Chihuahua. The Rio Bravo forms the border here, and it's one of the busiest

official crossing points between the two countries. There's clearly a great deal to see, as there is in any American city, but I have just one thing on my mind. As a cowboy trapped in the body of a comedian, it would be remiss of me to come to El Paso and not think about getting a new pair of boots.

WALK THE TALK: THE ROCKETBUSTER BOOT STORE

Ask anyone what footwear they associate with Texas and I think you'll get just one answer. I love a good pair of cowboy boots. Always have done. I'm well aware that some say the look is incomplete without a Stetson, but I don't have one of those because of something Keith Richards told me years ago. I'm not telling you what it is, but trust me when I say they're best left alone.

Cowboy boots are a different matter entirely. I've been wearing my favourite pair throughout this journey. They're complete with hand-tooled butterflies and a little birdie. I first had a pair made for me years ago. Back then, I used to spend a lot of time sitting in trailers on film sets and my wife would often come to visit. There would always be a per diem sitting on the table, money for food or whatever I needed that day. My wife would take one look and declare, 'That's dangerous! Anyone could steal it.' And I would never see it again. So one time I thought perhaps I should spend it, before she had the chance. I'd been leafing through a magazine called *Cowboys & Indians* and came across an advert for a made-to-measure service. One look at the pair in the picture, adorned with colourful hand-crafted imagery, and I saw my name written all over them. So I called them up and a very kind lady sent me special papers to draw my feet on. Following her precise instructions I sketched around my ankles, heel and instep and they went on to make a pair of boots I'm rarely seen without.

The bootmaker responsible, called Rocketbuster, is located here in El Paso. And like a salmon swimming upriver, I have brought my pair home. The square brick-fronted warehouse stands alone on the sidewalk, proud and independent, which sums up how I feel in their footwear. Inside, I meet the lovely lady who talked me through how to draw my feet. Co-owner Nevena greets me like a long-lost son and dips down to take a good look at how her babies are holding up. I think she can tell from the grin on my face that I love my boots, and yes, I tell her, they're just as comfortable as the day I first slipped them on.

'How did the business come about?' I ask, looking around at shelves of beautiful hand-crafted boots, tastefully complemented by retro kitsch and Western ephemera. It's a dream of a store.

'Well, my husband traded a '53 Cadillac Hearse for a wholesale boot company in a bar one night,' she says, and my attention snaps right back to her.

'As you do.' For a second, I wonder how my wife would respond if I did something similar. Nevena is beaming at me, and I figure she must be one in a million. Even so, I think out loud, How on earth did such a proposition come about?

'My husband used to work as a photographer back in New York,' she goes on, 'taking pictures for all the boot companies. They would show up with these great vintage boots, and he'd be like, "Oh, are you making these?" and they'd say, "No, we just want to shoot them for the cover." Now, my husband drove a Cadillac back then, and this guy in a bar fell in love with it. He offered to trade his boot company for the car, and that's how we went into business.'

Her husband felt like fate had just come knocking, Nevena tells me. As a collector of cowboy and science fiction memorabilia, he couldn't resist the name: Rocketbuster

'The next morning, he called up Roy Rogers and said, "I want to make boots just like you wore in the movies."'

'Roy Rogers the movie star?'

I've no idea whether Nevena notices that my eyebrows have hitched high, but she presses on merrily.

'So, he meets Roy, and the next thing you know they're best friends and my husband's in Roy's closet taking pictures.'

'You don't get more vintage than that,' I say.

'When we moved here from New York,' she goes on, 'I figured we could get much wilder with the styles, and then the whole thing just went nuts.'

On the subject of nuts, I spot a pair of boots embroidered with a fine-looking guitar on each back quarter. They look like they've been tattooed in the most exquisite way.

'I can't keep my eyes off them,' I say in sheer admiration.

Nevena looks around, her blonde hair whipping over her shoulder.

'I did those for Fender,' she says, and fetches them for me. 'It's based on the acoustic owned by Eddie Cochran, and the musical notes woven around it are from "Summertime Blues".'

'My God,' is all I can say, such is my awe, and it comes from the heart. The detailing is incredible. Through a combination of painting, studding, stitching and staining the leather boots in my hands feel like a work of art. Nevena shows me another pair featuring Buddy Holly's Stratocaster and musical notes from his hit song 'Rip It Up', and I am lost for words. It's fair to say customers are spoiled for choice when they venture here, and if they're anything like me they risk bankruptcy.

'What are the most exotic boots you've ever made?' I ask.

Nevena weighs up my question while scanning the shelves.

'These are Chinese dragons that wrap all around,' she says, and shows me a boot with a design that really should adorn a body. It looks totally organic, in line with the cut of the boot. I am entranced. 'I also did kitesurfers recently,' she says. 'Babe on boards with the ocean splash. People just ask for crazy stuff.'

I think of boot-wearing celebrities. As it turns out, I'm not short of suggestions.

'Did you do ZZ Top?'

'A long time ago,' she says casually. 'I've done Ethan Hawke and Julia Roberts.'

'Billy Bob Thornton?'

Nevena nods, and I wonder what design a guy like him might've gone for.

'Matt Damon,' she continues, looking dangerously like she could keep reeling off a list until closing time. 'Basically, you never know who is going to call.'

Next, I'm invited for a tour of the workshop area. Everyone present looks like they're delighted to be here, and I can see why. Nevena introduces me to Dee Dee on the finishing bench, Alisa on stains, Raoul handling stitching and Mannie the leather cutter 'with the dangerous prison knives'. Together, these masters of leatherwork are creating made-to-measure gems, with orders flocking in from around the world.

'This used to be an old trapper's warehouse,' Nevena tells me. 'It was built in the nineteen hundreds, and hides would've been hanging all over the walls. So, it sort of has a history in leather.'

The space is a wonderful mix of history, craftsmanship and art, and I find it dazzling. Every pair of boots in progress inspires me. Nevena shows me some more designs. I know from experience that she's skilled at teasing out just what each client has in mind, even if they're not confident in expressing it. I watch her pick out an image of a Day of the Dead skeleton, complete with the assembled bones of a little pup.

Cassandro's cape drops to the grass nonetheless, before he demurely takes the seat opposite me. In the world of *lucha libre*, which has a huge, passionate following in Mexico and many other Spanish-speaking countries, Cassandro is known as an *exótico* fighter. It's the second most popular sport after football, and this charming and impeccably polite man before me is considered the equivalent of a star striker.

'An *exótico* is basically a flamboyant fighter,' he explains. 'Way back in the day it was somebody who just played the gimmick of being gay, but since I came around, in 1987, I am what you see. I really am gay.' He stops to run a finger along the length of one eyebrow, smiling at me with teeth as white as bedsheets. 'One of my teachers gave me the name Cassandra but I was like, "I am *not* a woman, and I'm not one of those homosexuals that competes like a woman. I want to be Cassandr*o*." So, I bought the makeup, the pantyhose, the bathing suits and just glamorised a little bit of the wrestling. But of course, inside the ring, I'm a normal wrestler just like everybody else,' he stresses.

'Are there any other openly gay *lucha libre* wrestlers?' I ask.

Cassandro is pleased to confirm that he's not alone.

'There's a bunch of us now. We also have transgender people wrestling.'

'Really?' I'm surprised to hear this, but also rather delighted. For a sport that centres on macho aggression as much as theatrical drama, this strikes me as a pleasingly progressive fusion. Even so, I think to myself, surely there must be pockets of prejudice within the ring?

'Are there any holds that straight guys won't do with you?' I ask.

'I've been wrestling for twenty-seven years, so I'm very well respected,' he tells me. 'At first it was like, "Oh no, here he comes …"' Cassandro giggles and bats his lashes. Then he composes himself and tilts his chin upwards. 'Nowadays they bow to me,' he finishes with pride – and rightly so. 'I've been a world champion three times,' he adds.

I tell him that his courage is extraordinary. 'To stand up as a gay man in that world …' I say, and trail off there, because I'm lost for words. For Cassandro doesn't just strike me as being physically strong. There's an inner core of steel, I think.

'I went through a lot of rejection and discrimination in the early days, but that didn't define me. It defined them. And look at me now,' he finishes, with a flourish of his hands.

As if to demonstrate that his passion for the sport still burns as brightly as the day he began, Cassandro invites me to cross the park with him to a nearby practice ring. There, under a beating sun, a knot of men in trunks and masks take turns to spar and grapple. When Cassandro climbs through the ropes, without a mask as if he has nothing to hide, an air of reverence falls over them. *Lucha libre* might be carefully choreographed, and the slams and punches not quite what they seem, but afterwards Cassandro assures me that it's still physically punishing.

'I've had four surgeries on my knees,' he tells me on a break from flooring several opponents. 'Now my hands are giving up because of all my cervical damage,' he says, and clasps the back of his neck. 'As for my teeth, I've bought them like three times already because they got knocked out.'

'And everyone thinks it's a phony sport,' I say, chuckling at the irony.

'You can look at me right now and I'm very feminine,' says Cassandro, and then tightens one hand into a fist. 'Inside the ring, I'm a tough cookie.'

'Indeed.'

Cassandro doesn't need to show me his world title belts to prove this to me. I can see he's a formidable opponent. But for all the glamour and the face paint, I don't think he looks feminine at all, and I tell him that I mean that in the nicest sense. He strikes me as a gay man with far more courage than many people I've met, no matter what their sexuality or identity.

'Thank you,' he says, and I'm pleased he takes it as a compliment. 'I'm just a gay man. Being gay is a gift from God to me.'

'That's refreshing to hear,' I tell him. Then I remember reading a particular thing about him, and all of a sudden I'm desperate to learn his response. 'Cassandro, is it true you've been attacked by women?'

He nods solemnly.

'They think I'm beating up on their boyfriends, husbands, lovers or whatever,' he complains, 'and they just can't handle me. One time, this lady started screaming all these bad words at me. I turned around and I said, " Stop it, or you're going to get a heart attack!" I went, "Calm down, calm down!" and she got these nail clippers and just stabbed me right in my stomach.' Cassandro looks down at his taut abs, as if reliving the moment. And then he looks back up at me with vengeance in his eyes. 'I was like, "Oh no, you didn't"' – and he finishes with a mock punch in my face.

'You didn't!' I say, laughing despite myself. 'Did you?'

'Oh, hell yeah!' he crows. 'Popped her one!'

Despite the fact that I'm wincing at the details, I have to admire Cassandro's openness. I wonder how his family reacted when he first wrapped a feather boa around his neck and clambered into the ring.

'They've always been accepting of me,' he says, and he takes great joy in telling me about his siblings. 'In my family, we are three sisters, three brothers, three gay and three straight.' Then he mentions his father and his expression darkens by a watt. 'He never wanted anything to do with me until like six years ago,' he explains. 'We started talking and I told him I blamed him for everything, but that I had no need to forgive him because he didn't know any better. He just didn't know how to deal with me. He never told me that he loved me, or asked me how I was doing in school. It's that macho thing, but now he's my best friend. He's been through every surgery with me, and he's the last person I call when I leave and the first person I call when I come back. He takes care of my house and I just love that man,' he says with eyes that are beginning to shine, 'but we missed out on many years.'

'Is he proud of your success?' I ask.

Cassandro regains his composure and grins.

'I just found out that he has followed me through all of my life, even though he has never seen me in the ring because he says he wouldn't be able to see somebody beating me up. But you know, I think I'm in the last lap of my career. I seriously think I can't handle any more than another three years.'

'How old are you now?' I ask, thinking retirement in your twenties can't be fun. Cassandro tells me that he's forty-five, and my jaw falls. 'Really? You look amazing!'

'I'm glad to share it with you.' Cassandro's smile is blinding as he revels in the moment. His contribution to the sport and facing down prejudice clearly mean so much to him, and why not? Then he tells me that for several years he struggled with drugs and alcohol, and I sense that he considers overcoming this to be his greatest achievement.

'I've been clean for twelve years,' he says. 'That was ego, which is not my amigo, and I pray that I will walk in faith and beauty every day.'

I admire his convictions enormously. Cassandro is a fighter in every sense, but one with a great deal of soul. He rises to leave, presumably to return to coaching the next generation of *lucha libre* wrestlers.

'I'm deeply impressed by you,' I say, standing with him.

Cassandro is not a tall man by any stretch, and yet he overshadows me in other ways. His courage is just superhuman and I think he makes a great role model. To be a wrestler, a gay man in that world, takes guts, as it does to admit being hurt and broken. None of us are invincible, but we can all be true to ourselves.

'Thank you, sir,' he says, when I shake his hand, 'and may many more blessings come your way.'

I am disarmed by his humble charm, and grinning from ear to ear.

'Och, give us another cuddle,' I say, and spread my arms wide.

THREE

EL PASO TO NEW YORK

Continuing the theme of migration and dreams, this last stage of my giant loop around America by train is in some ways the most poignant and contemporary. It's about the final great wave of migration in the States and takes us towards the eastern seaboard, from the south up to the north.

This is a journey about music, race and the struggle against adversity – from the Cajun heart of Louisiana, through Birmingham, Alabama, where the city seeks to atone for its segregationist past; then on to the hard-boiled but always surprising seaport of Baltimore. And from there I have just one more stop to make – in the beating heart of the Big Apple.

About to leave El Paso, city of the finest cowboy boots and the nicest fighter in the world of *lucha libre* wrestling, I rejoin the *Sunset Limited*. Having come all the way from Los Angeles on the same train, it's beginning to feel like a second home. As well as the constantly changing view, I've come to appreciate the train's rhythm. So I settle back once more, as we push our way across epic vistas straight out of *Rio Grande* and *The Unforgiven*. The landscape is big in every sense and I suspect this mirrors the personalities of some of the good folk I'm set to meet. If my journey so far is anything to go by, I should prepare myself for anything.

The Lone
Star State

10

11

Louisiana

Alabama

12

13

Maryland

The End of
the Line

14

EXTRA TIME IN TEXAS

We're in the second-largest state of the United States of America. Alaska is larger, and effectively a country in its own right, but Texas isn't so far behind. It really is vast, covering over a quarter of a million square miles. So big, in fact, that the Lone Star State even stretches across two sections of this book. And it's my book, so why not, eh?

I've heard a great deal about San Antonio. It's effectively the gateway to the south-east of the USA and rich in history. It's abundant in natural history too, and there was one shot the director was desperate to get before we left town, so off he went to pay a visit to one of the biggest wonders in the state.

The Bracken Cave is located on the outskirts of the city and is really just a massive hole in the ground. And what is so fascinating about a cave, Billy? I hear you cry. And I'll tell you: bats.

Every summer, roughly twenty million of these creatures of the night flock here to roost. This makes it the largest known concentration of mammals in the world. Even more jam-packed than Brighton beach on an August bank holiday. You'd think they'd get on each other's nerves pretty quick and find somewhere else to hang out in the summer months, but apparently not. They must be laid-back little buggers, I deduce.

Now, we've all seen cave openings, but when you see this one I'm told it's out of the ordinary impressive. It was created by a sinkhole, which left what looks like a hundred-foot-wide mouth in a steep but shallow slope. I hope to God nobody was standing on the surface when the earth fell away because it looks bottomless. At dusk, however, something begins to stir within that black maw. In the last of the light as it glints off the odd wing. Then the first of the bats spirals out into the air. Within moments, a blanket of the wee creatures covers the sky. You might ask why I wasn't there to witness such a spectacle – well the prospect of a 4a.m. start to see them, and the potential of being soaked in bat urine as they emerge from the cave wasn't exactly my cup of tea I'm afraid!

I hear it's a breath-taking sight though, actually strangely hypnotic. It's as if you're not watching millions of bats, but one entity with masses of moving parts. It makes me think about humans and how we don't always interact so seamlessly for the greater good. We could learn a thing or two from these guys, I think to myself, before turning my mind to San Antonio for another mass event.

THE RULES OF THE GAME: HIGH SCHOOL FOOTBALL HIJINKS

Texans have three religions: God, barbecue and high school football. All three pillars of the state inspire widespread devotion, bringing people together from all walks of life. So, I've come to see for myself exactly how the sporting aspect binds the community.

It isn't just about the game, of course. On a Friday night, small communities all over Texas assemble to watch their local school teams duke it out on the pitch. We're not talking about a knot of dads on the touchline of the playing field, yelling obscenities at the referee. High schools like O'Connor in San Antonio take on their opponents at *stadium* level. This is a serious business. A place on the team makes any student a star pupil, while the rivalry is intense. In any given week, there are close to six hundred high school games across the state, featuring up to forty thousand players. Without doubt, high school football is huge here. It bookmarks the start of each weekend in the same way that Sundays are all about church. I make my way to the Farris Stadium, along with swarms of passionate disciples, to watch the American version of the beautiful game. When I smell burgers cooking on a griddle, I think perhaps I might be able to kill a Texan trinity of birds with one stone.

Now, I'll be honest, American football isn't my thing. Like so many Brits, I just don't understand it. I'm such a typical outsider, and though I've tried to make sense of the rules it always strikes me as involving a huge amount of effort for very little gain. This time, I've been invited to watch a local derby. The match, between the O'Connor Panthers and the Johnson Jaguars, is the equivalent of an Old Firm fixture, but with younger players and no drizzle. I take my place alongside the wife of the O'Connor coach, the delightful Lisa, and their two equally delightful daughters. We sit amidst seven thousand fans of the game that share a common bond: they all understand the rules of American Football and I don't.

As the match begins, featuring teams dressed up like assault squads, Lisa is quick to break down exactly what's happening and why. But through my eyes, the players move about six inches before the whistle blows to bring the action to a halt and replace it with a committee meeting. Every time, my host explains what's going on. I nod sagely, progressively none the wiser, until the half-time whistle blows. At least I *think* it's half-time. The whistle has sounded so often by then that I can't be sure. The only difference this time is that people are standing up.

'Wait until you taste the hot dogs!' says Lisa proudly, which earns my attention.

I'm hungry and eager to look around, so we head off to seek a stall.

I have to say, though I'm too polite to share this with my host, the hot dog I end up with is another dead duck, so to speak. It's a horror show, frankly: sprinkled with stale crisps masquerading as nachos and with cheese sprayed out of an aerosol. The cheese comes as a compulsory feature, which I would've declined given the chance, because it just sticks to my beard. As for the actual hot dog, which you'd expect to be huge given America's penchant for supersized food, frankly it looks more like a baby's penis. And tastes awful.

I also can't ignore the fact that some in this stadium are eating from buckets. I'm talking about popcorn and suchlike, but all the same this has always struck me as taking things too far. You should never eat anything that's served to you in a bucket. I would have thought that was obvious. Eating out of a bucket is for pigs, you know? It's one step away from going the whole hog and eating from a family trough – where all the food is laid out from one end to the other, everyone gathers around, gets down on their hands and knees and gorges away. What a hideous thought!

I was in a movie theatre once in Los Angeles. I asked for ice cream, because eating ice cream doesn't make any noise and disturb your fellow cinemagoers. But, no. They didn't have ice cream, but I could've ordered pizza and eaten it in my seat. There's even a little independent cinema near that one, which is lovely, except for the fact that you can buy stew to take into the auditorium. Stew! There really should be a law banning everything from movie theatres but ice cream. Whenever anyone sits down beside me with a bucket of food, the noise they make galloping it down is just horrible. The only proper use for a bucket, so I'm told, is that if you make a hole in the bottom you can push your willy through, offer it to the person next to you and give them a fright.

Buckets aside – and mercifully, nobody sitting next to me has one – the last thing I want to do is cast a downer on a sporting event that attracts so many devotees. American high school football may not be my preference, and I wouldn't recommend the half-time snacks, but the entertainment is second to none. Back in my seat, trying to lose the last of my hot dog under my feet, I watch with growing fascination as both sides unleash their marching bands onto the pitch. We're not talking about outfits half a dozen strong here. These are musical armies, with masses of cheerleaders, dancers and tumblers. And here's the thing: they don't have just one trumpeter, saxophonist or drummer. They have *squadrons*. Musically speaking, they're armed to the teeth! I count sixteen xylophone players, though you can't hear them as they're drowned out by the legion of trombonists.

What's more, as they march in formation across the pitch, the bands are playing jazz. Still smiling for my host and her daughters, I struggle not to reveal that I'm feeling a little deflated by it all. You don't get welders doing this sort of thing, d'you know what I mean? Still, despite all the pomp, and there is an awful lot of that, it's an opportunity to appreciate a lesser-spotted instrument: the sousaphone. Now, this is effectively a step up from the tuba, in that you get to wear it. Or it wears you, depending on how you look at it. Either way, the sousaphone is a smashing instrument, like a cross between a French horn and an anaconda. And I'm delighted to see both marching bands unleash their star players. These guys are picked, I'm sure, not so much for their playing skills but for their ability to actually shoulder their instruments. Under all those tubes of brass, the poor fellas look like they're trying to wrestle the things to the ground. After the misery of my hot dog, it really lifts my spirits.

The second half of the game arguably makes less sense than the first, but in such engaging company and after the hoot of watching the marching bands, I heartily enjoy the experience. It's just such a huge social thing. We're talking about a high school football match and yet *thousands* of people have turned up to watch. That half of them were in the bands is neither here nor there. It's very impressive for what is effectively an amateur football kickabout. Any Scottish Premier League fixture would kill to see numbers like they get here.

What sets these spectators apart is the fact that they don't chant or sing. Maybe they're too busy working out the rules. When one of the coaches pulls his team to one side and they hunker into a circle, I do wonder if the players are receiving a refresher course in what the hell is going on. To be fair, I wasn't looking forward to the game when I sat down at the start. When the final whistle blows, however, I realise I've had a marvellous time. As I file out with my hosts, it's clear to me that if I'm missing out on the magic, that's just my loss.

'It isn't only a game,' Lisa's husband David, the O'Connor Panthers' coach, tells me later. 'It's a rivalry between communities as well, but that's what unites everyone. They know us, we know them, and it's all about going out and giving all we've got, because there's no point in taking anything home with us.'

I admire David's outlook, as much as the fact that Texans understand what taking sides should be about. They don't use it as an excuse to beat seven shades out of each other, or anything like that. This is tribalism for all the right reasons. Some teams may be better than others, but in taking part we all become winners, and I applaud them for it. Without doubt, I leave with an understanding of the importance of the game in the tapestry of life here in the Lone Star state. And if the rules are beyond me, the spirit is crystal clear.

PLEASE BE SEATED: BARNEY SMITH'S TOILET SEAT MUSEUM

If you come to San Antonio, as I have done, people will besiege you with tales about the Alamo. The battle took place right here in 1836. And if you know nothing about the details, but talk to the locals, I can assure you that by the time you leave you'll be a leading expert on the subject. They're proud of their history, no matter what your view of it. It defines the city, and there's no escaping it even if you're just passing through.

The story is worth sharing, I should say. It marks a critical point in the Texas Revolution, in which American settlers within what was then a disputed Mexican province fought for independence. The Alamo itself was a former missionary compound that had been occupied by a small garrison of fewer than two hundred Texan soldiers. Amongst their number were Davy Crockett, the all-original King of the Wild Frontier, and Jim Bowie – so sharp with a knife they named one after him – a man of Scottish ancestry, I discover.

Inside the compound, Crockett, Bowie and their fellow soldiers came under siege from four thousand Mexican troops over the course of thirteen days. Although they were wholly outnumbered, they never surrendered. Finally, under the command of President General Antonio López de Santa Anna, the Mexicans attacked with unbridled ferocity. While the battle laid waste to the soldiers defending the compound, including Bowie and Crockett, the horror of the event served to galvanise people into joining the Texan army. Freshly strengthened in both numbers and spirit, the army repelled the Mexican forces within the space of a month. This brought an end to the revolution and saw Texas become an American state. It's a dramatic tale of passion and conflict that still polarises opinion, depending on what side of the border you're on. Within an hour of my arrival in San Antonio, on my way to see another famous site, I had absorbed enough information about the Alamo to make it my chosen subject in a quiz.

Davy Crockett and Jim Bowie are the names you're most likely to hear in San Antonio. Still, in keeping with my desire to shine a light on lesser-known individuals and places on my journey, I'm here to see the legacy of another son of Texas. You'll hear very little about Barney Smith, the plumber. He's a man who never fought in any battles, wore a funny hat or wielded a knife at anybody. But over the course of his life he's created a collection so unique that I feel duty bound to pay a visit.

In contrast to the drama of the Alamo, it's fair to say that Barney's work is a reflection of more pensive times. Not just in Texas but the world over. The museum he's created is located in a smart, tidy suburban street. It isn't hard to find. Walking past one detached house after another, I set eyes on the garage clad with toilet seats and feel pretty sure I've arrived at my destination.

Looking up and around, not just at the front of the garage but at every square inch of the interior walls, I find myself marvelling at the wall-hung loo seats and lids that serve as canvases for one man's unique brand of art. It's kind of a fitting pastime for a plumber, don't you think? They're even hanging in rows from the rafters, I see. All this creates a weird sensation like I'm stepping inside some kind of porcelain grotto. As well as using paints, Barney embeds objects including trinkets into his work, to create truly incredible mosaics. I'm drawn to seats studded with silver dollars, belt buckles and car registration plates. The registrations don't mean much to me, but I've no doubt they're significant to the artist, which is all that matters.

Now, Barney is in his nineties. Sadly, he isn't here in person to show me around, but that's understandable. I'm just grateful that he trusts me enough to let me look around and isn't worried that I might go mad and smash the place up, or something. There's little chance of that, in fact. Frankly, I'm entranced. Each seat is a work of art and a showcase for one man's creativity. How many of us would think that incorporating bow-ties into a toilet lid might work, and feel confident that a visitor like me would consider it to be just perfect? Moving deeper into this garage masquerading as a museum, with a central island of loo lids forming a circular passageway, I find one sporting all manner of cosmetic dentistry tools. It's inspired, but I'm not sure I'd like to see that kind of thing the moment before I park my bum. The same goes for the one carefully decorated with mirrors. I am drawn to the lid boasting tobacco pipes, however. To me, that's an invitation to sit down and just take your time. I don't know about you, but I should imagine some of my best ideas would come from parking my posterior on one of these.

There are over one thousand lids and seats in this collection, and counting. None of it is for sale. Barney has created this folk art purely for himself and for the pleasure of anyone who cares to pay a visit. There are no official opening times. Around here, Barney is famous for saying that he can be open within thirty minutes of someone calling to say they're on their way. Isn't that fantastic? What a guy.

As for the original concept, his father liked to hang trophy animal heads on the walls in the family home. Clearly, his son took a skewed look at the mounting boards, figured they looked a lot like toilet flaps, and decades later I'm here checking out his life's work. From peacocks fashioned from forks to London buses and Indian arrowheads, there's something for everyone here – assuming you buy into the basic concept.

As I make my way around the museum, heading back to the driveway and daylight, I spot several lids that Barney has created to commemorate moments in his life. The one featuring photos of him and his wife – she's looking quite

pleased – on their sixty-third wedding anniversary is a work of genius. In addition to the personal works and the playful and fun ones, some of Barney's lids are laden with a wider significance. I find one decorated with debris that washed ashore following the Challenger Shuttle disaster, another ingrained with volcanic ash from Mount Saint Helens, and even a loo seat that's said to have belonged to Saddam Hussein.

All in all, as I emerge blinking into the sunshine, smiling broadly, I have to admit it's a rather splendidly oddball collection. I'm always impressed that when ordinary things are amassed in this way they attain a kind of grandeur, you know? And Barney Smith is a true collector and artist because he does it all for himself. He doesn't care what people think, and I speak from experience.

I used to collect snow globes as a kid. I didn't tell anyone for a while. Then I decorated my room with them, people saw them and liked them. But it wasn't their response that fired me up, it was the fact that I had taken an ordinary, banal object and made it significant by having so many. As a result, I have a weakness for seeking out other people's collections, no matter what they are of. I've met someone who collects ice-cream cones and a guy from Fife who has an amazing haul of toy space guns. One toy gun looks totally ordinary, but thirty-nine in one place are instantly *spectacular*. I can't resist it. If someone calls me at home and says they've heard about a collection of Ethiopian ear picks, I'll drop everything and rush out to see it. As well as the transformative effect of seeing the same thing in multiple variations, I think it speaks volumes about the collector and what makes them tick. It's like a scrapbook of their life and a testament to their individuality.

I may not have had the pleasure of meeting Barney Smith, the man behind the finest collection of toilet seats the world has ever seen, but I salute him.

LOUISIANA

I'm on the move again, and back on board the *Sunset Limited*. This is set to be my tour of the deep South, and I'm looking forward to it immensely. Texas has been a treat, but now it's time to move on from the canyons, prairies and plains, and lose ourselves in the swamps, creeks and bayous of the neighbouring state and beyond.

Much of Louisiana's distinctive landscape is down to the tail end of the Mississippi River. As the sediment washed down from this mighty waterway, it created a huge network of deltas and marshland, while the rich mineral content seeded dazzling flora and wildlife. Throw in the savannahs and the dense pine forests and you have a state like no other. I can appreciate this for myself from the train. One of the great joys of travelling in a relatively straight line is the

213

fact that we plunge across terrains of every description. It serves up a very clear picture of how the country locks together geographically. As we close in on our next destination, the city of Lafayette, there can be no doubt we're in one of the most exotic regions that America has to offer.

MUSIC AS MEDICINE: THE OFFSHORE LOUNGE

I've come to Lawtell, a small town north of Lafayette, to see a shack. These may be commonplace around here – though this one might be extra large – but most notably it's home to a musical phenomenon. The Offshore Lounge is tucked away behind the main highway, near the railway crossing and the service station. In stifling heat, I'm greeted by the sound of cicadas, a dog barking in the distance, and the muffled but unashamedly joyous sound of a performance from within this unassuming clapboard building.

Louisiana is the birthplace of Cajun music. It's a form of balladry that calls upon so many influences that the overall sound is unique. To understand this musical melting-pot we have to go back to the 1700s, when exiled French colonists from Canada – known as Acadians – arrived here to make a new home. Legend has it that the first thing they did when they stepped off the boat was to offer up a prayer of thanksgiving … and then they danced. As the Acadians established their culture and absorbed other ethnic groups around them, so a distinctive form of music was forged. The influence of Cajun – a corruption of 'Acadian' – reaches far and wide, from Country and Western to contemporary pop.

Best of all, however, is a traditional offshoot with a distinctive Creole influence: zydeco. The word is supposedly a shortening of a Creole French phrase meaning 'the beans aren't salty', and I really hope that's true. It's a reference to being so poor that you couldn't salt the pork commonly used to season food, while the music itself is notably upbeat in order to lift the spirits. Isn't that wonderful?

On stepping inside the Offshore Lounge and allowing a moment for my eyes to adjust, I listen to three musicians in full swing. Two are playing accordions.

Another brushes, flicks and scrapes an infectious rhythm from a washboard. It's fast-paced and foot-stomping stuff, with a touch of blues in the vocal delivery and down-on-your-luck lyrics. I'm sure zydeco aficionados will be quick to point out the presence of the two-step and the shuffle and whatnot. From a visitor's perspective, this is music played with heart, soul and sheer joy. As the trio come to a close, I cross the floor to meet them, with a mile-wide grin across my face.

'That was superb!' I say, and pump their hands in turn.

'How you doin', sir?'

The Bayou Swamp Band's leader, Chubby Carrier, clasps his accordion and proudly introduces me to his fellow musicians: brother Dickie and cousin Neil. All three are achingly polite, like old-school gentlemen, but also full of laughter and life. I am made to feel very welcome, which is entirely in keeping with the spirit of the club, as founded by Chubby's father, Roy.

A former oil worker in the Gulf of Mexico, Roy Carrier opened the club in the early Eighties. It was intended as a place where he and his extended family could gather during holiday periods, to jam and play out their passion for zydeco. Word quickly spread and the rest is history. For years, the Offshore Lounge, named after the location of Roy's former workplace out on the rigs, attracted fans from across the state, the country and then the world. With its open-door policy and plenty of good food and drink on offer, this was a dance hall I just wish I could've experienced in its heyday. Chubby is a multi Grammy-award winning zydeco musician, and he and his family have had a huge influence on the zydeco music scene, but the fact is that Chubby, his brother and their cousin are playing today for an audience of one. Sadly, when Roy passed away the family were faced with certain health and safety demands along with costs they couldn't meet, so they were forced to make the heartbreaking decision to close the club. But I'm not here to focus on what was clearly such a sad moment in their lives. The music I just heard couldn't fail to make your heart soar, and I want to know much more.

'It must take you back, playing here,' I say.

Chubby draws breath to respond and for a second I think he's struggling to find the right words.

'Oh, it does,' he says with a sigh. 'You know, we miss those days. I was fifteen when I first got in this club, just coming up as a boy. And to think about all the great music that's been here: my father's music, my grandfather's music, as well as all my relatives that played here back in the day. It brings back memories. And those days, I tell you what, I wish that I could bring them back.'

It must be tough, I think, for Chubby to reflect, in this building that has clearly seen better days. It's gloomy and dilapidated, and yet having heard them play it's no stretch for me to picture the place rammed to the rafters with party-loving people hell-bent on letting off steam. It's said that when things got really wild the building would actually shake.

'Is that true?' I ask, but I can tell from the way the three chuckle that it's possibly something of an understatement.

'My father would have to go under the floor and prop it up with bricks,' laughs Chubby. 'He said, "If it ain't shaking, nobody's having a good time."'

'Did you help?'

'Oh, sure. Him and I went under this club several times, to brace it together.'

The Offshore Lounge is basically a big barn. Judging by the way the floor creaks, it may be even less sturdy than it used to be.

'Weren't you frightened?'

'We had to fix it,' he says with a shrug, as if a little personal risk was a small price to pay to keep the party going.

Since his father and grandfather were both zydeco legends, I ask Chubby when the music first became a way of life for him.

'Well, I joined my daddy's band when I was ten years old,' he says.

'Ten?'

I'm astonished. That's quite an age for any wee lad to be taking to the stage, with or without grown-ups.

'Daddy was always in debt for a drummer,' he tells me, using a poignant turn of phrase. 'At home, I'd beat on my momma's pots and pans, and that's when he said: "Boy, you need to get back there and start playing on those drums." I didn't know all his music, but I heard what he did at rehearsal and so I just filled in behind. Then one time the drummer he had didn't show up. Daddy said to his guitar player, a guy called Mitson: "You know what? You need to go and get Chubby."'

'Where were you?' I ask, enjoying this story immensely.

'I was in the yard, playing football with my friends. Now old Mitson had a stutter. He comes round and said: "Ch-ch-ch-ch-ch-Chubby …" I said: "What's up man?" He said: "Y-y-y-your daddy needs you." "For what?" I asked. 'T-t-to play the drums?" I was one happy kid!' he adds, as I laugh along with Dickie and Neil, and figured Mitson would've got his own back somehow. 'I made a beeline to the club,' Chubby continues. 'I got to the door, and there's this man looking at me standing tall, and he said: "Hey, lad! What you doing here?" I peered up at him and replied: "Oh, I came to play the drums with my daddy." My daddy saw me and said: "Hey, John, let him in! That's my son. He gonna play the drums." The guy looked back at me and said: "That little kid?" And that's how I got the gig with my Daddy.'

I love how Chubby tells this story. Not just that it's a coming-of-age tale, but the rapid-fire rate at which he tells it, switching from one voice to the next. He's a natural-born entertainer, and I'm delighted when they offer to play me another song. For a boy who earned his musical chops playing drums for his dad, I'm struck by the fact that Chubby is a natural with the accordion. He plays instinctively, never looking at the instrument, but maintaining eye contact with his band mates throughout. All of them play with big smiles that never falter.

'Tell me about that,' I say afterwards, and point at his accordion.

Chubby peers down like a proud father with a newborn in a sling.

'Well, it was sitting at home,' he begins. 'Back in the day we never had PlayStations and all that stuff, you know? We had instruments in our house. My grandfather used to play the accordion on the front porch all the time for us. He was a sharecropper. He'd get off of work, and then right after supper he'd grab his accordion and go sit on the porch. And I can hear his old foot, he was stompin' hard. I'd ask him: "Where you getting this music from?" and he would say: "Oh, I have a lot of troubles in my life. I can't afford a psychiatrist or anything like that, so I sing the blues away, I sing my troubles away." I said: "So, you're telling me that music is your medicine?" My grandfather would reply: "This accordion is the best medicine I can get!" My Daddy would play it in his band, too. But when he had to go to work he'd leave it behind. As a kid, bored out of my mind, I just picked it up one day and started playing. My Daddy heard me, and he said: "Hey, you like that accordion?" I said: "Yes, I do!" One Christmas, he bought me my very own accordion. And that day I became the third generation of my family to become a zydeco accordionist.'

Chubby tells me that he thinks about his late grandfather and his father every time he picks up the instrument, which is lovely. Isn't that a brilliant way to honour past generations? Just listening to him brings home to me what a powerful and binding force music can be.

'I'm still going at it,' he tells me. 'It's in my blood. I mean, I can't *stop* playing. I love it! If I'm in the office, doing work, sometimes I'm like: Oh, my God, I'm going crazy today! So, I go sit on my back porch, play my accordion and think my grandfather was right all along. Music is my medicine! When I was growing up, in my younger days, I wouldn't relate to that. But as I got older, and had a family of my own, I said to myself: I'm going to do what my papa did. I'm gonna sing my troubles away.'

Hearing Chubby Carrier & the Bayou Swamp Band play for me once again, and feeling that sense of elation once again, I can't help feeling I have found the heart of Louisiana. I may be alone in enjoying this moment, but it's easy to see how this infectious brand of music could've whipped up a gathering.

'Every Thursday night,' Chubby tells me, when I ask how often the Offshore Lounge was open. 'Yeah, that's how we used to do it. Daddy used to bring a lot of bands here to rehearse, and really that's how it started off. People outdoors would hear the music. They'd come to the door and they look in and my Daddy would say: "Ahh we're not open, we're just rehearsing." And then he started thinking: "Hmm …" So before you know it the rehearsals became a Thursday night zydeco jam session. All the musicians from all the surrounding areas came to the Offshore Lounge. And a lot of those guys got their starts right here at the sessions.'

I adore hearing how small ventures turn into worldwide sensations, often by chance, and this is one such tale. Chubby himself has enjoyed great success with his band, playing to audiences around the world. I come away feeling it's a tragedy that the Offshore Lounge was forced to close its doors. The place just lies empty, which is the saddest thing. Chubby informs me that plans are afoot to renovate the building and I hope to God they make that happen. It's a shame that enthusiasm alone can't restore the place, because it would be back up to speed in a blink. If it hadn't been shut down by red tape, I believe they'd still be running at full capacity.

Sometimes I think we should be allowed to make our own decisions around safety issues. A long time ago, I used to go to a club run by a member of the Incredible String Band. It was held on a fourth floor and always packed. But the only way up and down was by elevator. There were no rules against it back then, but if there'd been a fire, we'd have been barbecued. Everyone was well aware of that risk and yet they showed up of their own free will and enjoyed a great night out. We should be given more choice in this sort of thing. I just hope that while the Offshore Lounge is closed those musicians will return to their back porches to soothe their troubles and inspire the next generation to master the medicinal art of zydeco.

SWAMP THING: IN COMPANY ON THE BAYOU

I wasn't born on the bayou, in accordance with that great Creedence Clearwater song. I come from Glasgow, and as I speed across this open stretch of Louisiana waterland, I can tell you now it has an entirely different kind of vibe. I don't pass bookmakers and chip shops here but swathes of semi-submerged cypress trees. Wading birds perch in the branches and watch us flash by.

I'm in classic Cajun country now and feeling the part. With a belly full of crawfish pot pie and my neckerchief twisted into a headband to keep my hair at bay, I'm seated at one side of this little boat while resisting the urge to trail

my hand through the water. I've seen enough movies about this isolated neck of the woods to know that certain reptiles might be lurking. My pilot for this trip *surely* looks the part, and he should be an expert tour guide of the waterways around here. The wonderfully named Coerte A. Voorhies stands behind the wheel at the back as we zip along, seemingly deaf to the roar of the engine. It's a colossal noise. I wonder if he might *really* be deaf as a result. For a while, as we navigate through this watery woodland, crossing big open stretches from time to time, I am content to feel the wind on my face and bask in the sunshine. I close my eyes for a moment, but then my man powers down the engine and we slow to a gentle chug.

'This is the bayou,' he says.

I look around. We're in a channel flanked by thick undergrowth. From an outsider's point of view, it strikes me as being no different from the last few miles, but Coerte speaks with great authority. He's wearing a duck-billed cap pulled so low over his sunglasses that he's really only visible from the nose down. His goatee, as white as snow and clearly catching on, tells me this guy is seasoned enough to know a thing or two about our environment. 'Bayou is an Indian word,' he continues. 'It literally means "small river".'

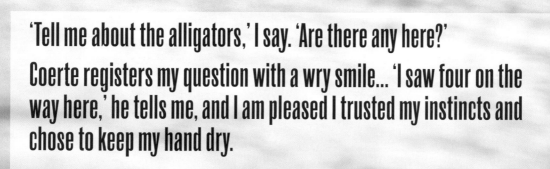

'Tell me about the alligators,' I say. 'Are there any here?'

Coerte registers my question with a wry smile... 'I saw four on the way here,' he tells me, and I am pleased I trusted my instincts and chose to keep my hand dry.

'This is small?'

To British eyes it's as far from the concept of a small river as you can possibly imagine. It looks more like a national park in the thrall of a biblical flood. Coerte tells me what I'm looking at now is nothing.

'We've lost a lot of water recently,' he says, leaning on the wheel. 'Up until eight weeks ago, we had eight feet of it in these trees. If you look closely, you can see the watermark.'

It's an odd thing to see a tideline in these upper branches, and a measure of how swiftly water can move in wetlands known for copious rainfall. A white ibis peers down at me like I've done something wrong.

'How do these trees survive with so much water?' I ask.

'They just acclimatise,' says Coerte, who is equally unruffled by the bugs buzzing around us. 'The cypress has two nemeses: the axe and lightning. Those trees with the tops broken off?' he adds, and I can see several that look like spent and splintered matches. 'They got hit.'

With just the sound of the motor ticking over now, it's eerily quiet. I look around, wondering what other threats might be present. I wouldn't care to be out here in a thunderstorm, but it's what might be lurking below the surface of the water that continues to beggar my imagination.

'Tell me about the alligators,' I say. 'Are there any here?'

Coerte registers my question with a wry smile. It's as if he's been expecting me to ask it for some time.

'I saw four on the way here,' he tells me, and I am pleased I trusted my instincts and chose to keep my hand dry.

He explains that when the sun goes down they come out in force.

'With a powerful spotlight you'd be surprised how many you can see,' he says. 'Literally hundreds.'

I look around one more time. The fact that I can see no sign of life beyond the birds and the bugs is deeply disconcerting.

'Do they really have red eyes?' I ask, because I've heard this said but I'm not sure if it's a myth to make them sound like demons.

'Like ruby lasers,' confirms Coerte, which frankly gives me the willies. He casts his eye along the waterline, lost in thought for a moment. 'There are upwards of three million in the neighbourhood. For a number of years we protected them. Then they started breeding properly. That's when we "upped our backsides" as the old saying goes, and the 'gators knew it.'

As he speaks, I half expect a monster of the deep to rise out of the water behind him. In the absence of a giant alligator attack, I think of the only song I know about the beasties.

'"Polk Salad Annie",' I say, and a flash of recognition comes into Coerte's eyes, 'The 'gators got your grannie.'

'That's the one,' he says.

'We don't have songs like that in Scotland,' I add. 'Although we do have one about how difficult it is to shove your granny off a bus.' Coerte smiles politely at me, but I know a baffled man when I see one. 'Generally where I come from there's no risk of being eaten by an alligator,' I continue anyway. 'Except in very dangerous parts of Edinburgh.'

As we're gliding along at a gentle pace, Coerte has every opportunity to change the subject onto more familiar ground.

'See the pink bird,' he says, sounding relieved, and nods towards a glade of land between the trees. I turn to see the object of his attention, a wader, sunning its wings in the shallows. It's sensationally beautiful, with feathers the colour of candyfloss and against a backdrop that could be a stage for a ballet. 'That's a spoonbill.'

I remark on how little dry land there appears to be. As we round a bend in the bayou and pass several houseboats that Coerte tells me belong to deer hunters, I'm left thinking that I just haven't been looking hard enough.

'Are there really deer in there?' I ask, straining to see through the tangle of undergrowth.

'Deer, cougars, black bear, red wolves.'

'Get out of here!'

I twist around once more to face him directly.

'There's a lot of high, dry land in there,' he assures me. 'Even when we have high water, you can see coyotes, raccoons, possums, mink, otter and beaver.'

This comes as a revelation to me. At the same time, there's something about the landscape that leaves me with the distinct impression that I'm being watched. Not only that, but whatever has you in their sights is moving along through the foliage keeping up with you. Maybe I really have seen too many movies, but at any moment I expect a man to pop up out of the undergrowth with a blowpipe between his lips.

'Does anyone live here?' I ask.

3

'In the days before we had fast boats,' says Coerte. 'There are maybe a few characters who choose to stay hidden. Those guys like to booze and stay drunk without anyone bothering them. But the last one I knew is dead now.'

It's with some relief on my part that Coerte squeezes the gas at this point and we motor onwards. Maybe he knows something, I think, but soon find myself occupied by the water. It's so still that it reflects the foliage on both banks with perfect symmetry and makes this channel feel even narrower than it really is.

'How about fish?' I ask. 'I imagine there's a lot.'

'This is Louisiana's answer to the Grand Canyon,' he says. 'It's full of good fishing, and a more beautiful spot than you will ever see.'

As a keen angler, I am yearning to cast a line over the side of the boat. If there's plentiful wildlife watching us from the shoreline, I'm pretty sure I'd have a lot of success with my landing net here.

A few minutes later, I'm left to wonder whether I'd even need a net when a large fish leaps clean from the water nearby. A confident catch with my hands would probably do the job.

'Whoa!' I say and gasp at the sight, for the fish looks like it's just been detonated from the depths. 'What was that?'

'Asian carp,' say Coerte casually, with barely a glance in the direction of the splash as the fish plunges back down. 'They were kept in farms to feed on algae, but got loose in the big flood of 1978. As one female can lay up to two million eggs each year we're up to our backsides in them.' With one hand on the wheel, Coerte keeps a steady pace through the water. Then another fish leaps from our path, followed swiftly by another. 'They go crazy when they hear the engine,' he explains.

'Do they taste good?'

Coerte tells me that he likes them on his grill.

'We have a French chef down in Baton Rouge who calls them "silver fin",' he says. 'Americans don't like the word "carp". Switch one letter and you know what you get?'

It takes me a second to figure it out and I laugh with him. My smile is wiped from my face, however, when another big carp flicks into the sky as if the water has just been electrified. Only, this one lands in the boat.

'Jesus!'

While I react like the maid in *Tom and Jerry*, Coerte stands between me and the giant fish as if to protect me from attack.

'I'd say that's about a thirty-pounder,' he comments, as it flips and slaps about in the hull. 'You don't want to get hit in the face by one,' he warns me. 'It could kill you.'

With great expertise, Coerte collects the floundering carp and eases it over the side. As I watch the fish slip away, I can't help thinking it landed in the boat on purpose.

'Why would it do that?' I ask, when Coerte agrees that it does sometimes appear that way.

I am genuinely flummoxed. Are these fish evolving into kangaroos? Animals don't do this kind of thing without a reason, after all. What do they think will happen when they flip out of the water? It must be something in their DNA, I reason to myself. Maybe they imagine something else will be on board, like a giant mother fish with her arms open to suckle them. As the sun begins to drop behind the cypress trees, darkening the water by the minute, I decide that maybe I'll never know. All I can say is that if you landed a carp like the one that just presented itself to me you'd be well pleased. No doubt you'd wear out your camera phone taking pictures of it.

By the time my excitement at coming close to being battered to death by a flying carp has subsided, I realise that dusk has seriously set in.

'We'd better get back,' mutters Coerte, which sounds good to me, though it's his tone of voice that also makes me think hanging around in the bayou might not be the best idea. So I ask him outright if there's a reason and then half wish I'd just settled back for a peaceful return to base.

'Do you know who Rougarou is?'

'No.'

'A Cajun werewolf.'

'Oh,' I say.

'You don't want to mess with one, or be out here after the sun is down completely, because they are *bad*!'

I listen quietly as Coerte tells me the legend of this fearsome creature that's said to stalk the swamps. With a human body and the head of a wolf, Rougarou is often summoned as a means of encouraging children to behave. By the time Coerte finishes the story and the sun's last gleaming retreats behind the horizon, I assure him that I won't cause any trouble if he'll just take me back to civilisation.

I have a train to catch, after all.

FROG CITY: THE QUEENS OF GREEN

There are times when you hear about a city's reputation and think 'I have to go there!' Rayne is one such city, just east of Lafayette in Louisiana. So, what does it have to offer? It's the frog capital of America. See? I said you'd want to visit.

It's the swamps surrounding Rayne that are responsible. Once upon a time, bullfrogs thrived in the warm, watery and bug-rich environment. The local folk were quick to catch on to the fact that in certain parts of the world the legs were considered a delicacy. In the twentieth century, they actually exported stocks to the restaurants of Paris, who were proud to offer *The best frog legs from Rayne, Louisiana, the Frog Capital of the World* on their menus. They even took off across the USA, to become the city's most valuable export. Imagine that? Frogs.

Things aren't what they used to be, however. Over the years changing culinary tastes, stiff competition and a less robust local frog population have put Rayne's most celebrated industry out of business. But the residents are still immensely proud of their heritage, and I'm keen to find out more.

Even if I came here with no prior knowledge of Rayne, I'd get a strong sense that frogs have played a significant role in its history. This is largely down to the frog statues. There are one hundred and ten in total. I learn the number from my wonderful guide, Suzette, from the city council. I'm not entirely sure of her precise job description, but she has a huge, easy and infectious laugh, and I'd employ her on the strength of that alone. I'm also in no doubt that she's a treasure trove of frog trivia.

'They'd load the frogs onto trains,' she tells me as we amble through a local park. 'That's how we shipped them right up to the 1970s.'

I tell her it's clear the city wears its heritage on its sleeve. Suzette takes this as her cue to expand on just how far Rayne takes its celebration of the humble frog.

'We have a frog festival every year,' she says. 'And there are some frog queens who are dying to meet you. We also have a little frog derby. Would you be interested in racing frogs with us?'

I've only just met Suzette. If she'd known me for a minute longer she'd also know for sure that I am dying to go frog racing. Just then, it feels like the whole purpose of my existence has suddenly been revealed to me.

'Show me the way,' I tell her.

It was a Parisian by birth, one Jacques Weil, who was to make his name here during the golden age of the frog trade. He arrived in America sometime in the late 1890s, settled in Rayne and found initial success – alongside two business associates – with a general store called Boudreaux, Léger and Weil.

Over time, the store built a reputation for specialising in wilder commodities. Weil did a good trade in pecans and furs, but then bullfrogs became a big deal on the dinner table and demand went through the roof. Weil wasn't responsible for the introduction of frogs' legs as a delicacy, but he was passionate about the product. Thanks to him, word about the quality of Rayne's frogs spread far and wide.

Behind the store, he built a large chicken-wire cage. This 'frog aquarium' held up to fifteen thousand of the little green beasties – gathered from the swamps – and kept a five-man cleaning crew busy. Bright lights above the cage attracted insects at night, and provided the condemned amphibians with their final meal before their fateful rendezvous with the skinning knife.

Jacques Weil did not believe in waste. Legend has it that when his skinners arrived at work and found that some of the caged frogs had suffocated overnight, their employer urged them: 'Kill the dead ones first!'

Weil himself passed away in 1948, just over two decades before the demand for Rayne's frogs began to dwindle. By then, however, they had graced fine dining tables around the globe. Thanks to a NASA experiment, a handful even ended up in space. Today, a small trade lives on, supplying schools and colleges with frogs for dissection. It's a sad end to a glorious tale, but my guide is determined that my visit shall be a joyous occasion. And when I say joyous, I mean surprising and a wee bit surreal.

'We're off to meet the mayor,' Suzette tells me as we cross to a pavilion in the park where the man himself is waiting. 'He'd like to declare that today is Billy Connolly Day!'

We shake hands. I am genuinely touched and a little baffled, but there's no time to check there hasn't been some hideous misunderstanding.

'We have a proclamation, for you,' he says, and invites me to follow Suzette to the other side of the pavilion. There, waiting in the sunshine, a small crowd greets me. Many are wearing sashes and tiaras. The frog princesses, I presume. I notice some are clutching frogs. One frog is sporting a tiny top hat. With no time to even pinch myself, I stand alongside the mayor. Solemnly, he begins to read from a posh-looking script.

'I hereby recognise Billy Connolly as an honorary citizen of the city of Rayne,' he begins, 'and extend to him this certificate of appreciation for his interest in our community with the most cordial invitation to visit at any time. Further I do hereby assure him that he has made an excellent choice in choosing this community as his adopted city. It is a token of our thanks for showing the world what we have to offer here in Rayne, Louisiana. So this is for you …'

I'm so stunned by this turn of events that it takes me a second to take the key from the mayor's hand. Squinting into the sunshine, I clear my throat. Had I known this was going to happen, I'd have prepared a speech. Instead, I have no choice but to busk it.

'Thank you very much for accepting me as a member of your city,' I begin. 'And I promise not to use my key to come and peep into your houses when you least expect it.'

It's hardly the Gettysburg address, but my words are met with a fluttering of applause. With the ceremony over, and the freedom to do what I please across Rayne's four quarters, I choose to behave myself by inviting Suzette to enlighten me further about the frogs. We don't have to travel far. In fact, the frogs come to us, along with their handlers who I had spotted in the audience.

'We have some beautiful frog derby queens,' she tells me, and beckons several young ladies from the crowd. Each one carries a little plinth with a frog on board, including the one with the spiffy headwear. 'If ya'll come forward,' Suzette continues, 'we would like you to judge them and see which one you like the best.'

I am introduced in turn to the girls and their frogs. The girls smile and tell me their names. The frogs eye me with penetrating focus, as if they've been in training for this event for months. As well as the entrant in a top hat, who is called Infrognito, I learn, I am faced with a frog in a mock front room, complete with a tiny TV set tuned to a sports channel. The third one sits on a plinth divided by a tennis net. He's called Deuce, which takes me a second.

'How are they to hold, then?' I ask, because each girl is supporting her plinth with one hand and gently clasping the frog to stop it from hopping off.

In response, all three young princesses smile at me beatifically. Suzette summons the girl holding the tennis-playing frog. I follow her instruction and carefully take the little player from her. I'm not sure how it feels about being all dressed up. Probably the same as I do holding it.

'Would you like to take one home with you?' asks Suzette.

I hand the frog back to the princess.

'No, thank you,' I say politely.

'Well, we'll get some pictures of you with them. How about that?'

I tell her that I'd love to do that. I join the girls for a photograph. Suzette looks on with a smile as bright as the Louisiana sun above.

'I think they're trying to meet their prince, what do you think? Maybe that's why they play with the frogs.'

'Is there a lot of frog kissing going on around here?' I ask her.

'That's right.' Suzette flicks her eyes at the girls and back to me, as if kiss-and-tell tales are off limits, but her smile doesn't waver by a jot. I sincerely hope that as a freeman of the city I haven't come as a disappointment to them. 'Awesome,' she says for good measure, as the camera flash goes off.

Afterwards, I am asked to make one of the toughest decisions of my life. The three girls line up with their fancy-dress frogs and I'm asked to choose the winner. They've all made a huge effort and the frogs have been so well behaved, and so for that reason I make my pick based on names alone.

'It has to be Infrognito,' I say, and a ripple of applause washes over the audience.

There's another reason why Suzette has been so keen to crown the winner. It means all three entrants to the frog fancy-dress competition can be disrobed in preparation for their next event: the frog race. She ushers the girls away to get them ready and I seriously wonder whether they might return in running shorts and vests. Until then, Suzette has other plans to ensure this is a visit I'll never forget.

'I'd like to introduce you to another set of frog festival royalty,' she says, as a trio of tiara-toting young ladies step in from the sidelines. As well as their sashes and crowns, all three are dressed in frog green. Suzette, bursting with pride, gestures for them to come closer. 'The girls compete to hold beauty titles. We have different age divisions,' she adds, and prompts one of the older girls to take over.

'I'm Carly,' she says, and drops her gaze. 'From the Unmarried Division.'

'And I'm the new teen festival queen!' The girl beside her seems way more enthusiastic about her title, as does the Junior Prom Queen and Dana, from the Married Division. I feel awfully sorry for Carly.

Suzette, however, has saved the best until last. She now makes way for a senior couple in buttercup-yellow sweatshirts, sashes and sparkling crowns.

'This is our golden age frog festival King and Queen,' she says. 'Meet Michael and Alice!'

'We're the *old* king and queen,' says Michael.

'Not old,' Alice says to correct him. 'Just golden.'

'Well, I'm exceptionally old,' I tell them. 'Feel free to be old.'

Once again, Suzette moves things along at a terrifying lick.

'The great thing about these ladies and gentlemen is that they represent Rayne all over the state. They attend numerous festivals and city events throughout Louisiana and promote tourism in our city. They're ambassadors, and they do a great job.'

As a concept, calling upon frogs to bring prosperity to a place strikes me as bonkers but wonderful. I am completely sold. When Suzette tells me that the fancy-dress frogs have now completed their transformation into racing frogs, I cannot wait to see them in action.

'Show me how it's done,' I say, as the girls return with their competitors in buckets.

'We're gonna give you a little stick,' says Suzette.

I take the stick from her and weigh it in my hand.

'You don't hit them, do you?'

Suzette hoots with laughter and assures me that they don't. By now, a man in a yellow jerkin called Luke has stepped up to oversee the proceedings. With great politeness, he asks if I would mind taking a step back because I am standing on the start line.

'You probably won't need the stick because they're pretty lively,' he says. 'It's only for a gentle poke if your frog gets a little stubborn.'

With a measuring tape in hand, Luke goes on to instruct me that each frog is judged on the best of three jumps.

'What am I doing here?' I ask myself quietly, as one of the frog derby queens settles her competitor behind the line.

'OK,' says Luke, as she stands back with bated breath. 'And … go!'

Sensing freedom, no doubt, the first frog makes a hop for it. Not three times but four. Luke is quickly on the scene, scooping up the runaway before it reaches the shrubbery. The drama is over in a matter of seconds, but causes quite a scene.

Meanwhile, sensing an opportunity, another of the frogs escapes from its bucket and begins to hop madly in the opposite direction.

'Runaway frog!' cries Suzette, and despite her unwavering smile I detect panic in her voice.

With all the frogs accounted for and the handlers regrouped, the derby continues. After one of the younger queens, Victoria, gives it a shot, Suzette summons her mother. This is Holly, who tells me she won the competition way back in 1991. As she does so, her frog breaks for the border. The flower border, I should add, and he very nearly makes it. Once again, to peals of nervous laughter from Suzette, bedlam breaks out. I am content to watch these frog-crazed residents run around trying to restore order. Then Luke approaches me with a bucket and I realise my moment has arrived.

'Just place him on the starting line there, Billy,' he says. 'And just give him a gentle poke.'

I follow his instructions and just touch the frog's rear quarters with the tip of my stick. It responds by doing absolutely nothing, much to hoots of mirth from my host. And then, without warning, he's off. Sideways. And as it turns out, I make third place!

'Good job,' Luke tells me, but I'm not sure I can claim the credit.

In second place it's young Catherine, but the winner – and it clearly means a great deal to her after a winning drought of more than two decades – is Holly.

'How do you feel about your mum winning?' I ask Catherine, as Holly soaks up the applause.

'It's a little upsetting,' she admits.

An awkward silence descends upon us, which just confirms how seriously they take these things in Rayne. Suzette picks up on the atmosphere in a heartbeat and is quickly at my side.

'Now I have a question for you,' she says. 'Have you ever eaten frog legs?'

I tell her that I have, and very nice they were too, but privately I'm not entirely sure this is the time or the place. So I politely decline Suzette's kind invitation to visit a nearby restaurant, and instead turn my attention to congratulating the winner.

'What happens to the frogs now?' I ask Holly, newly crowned as the derby queen.

'We release them into the wild,' she says, which pleases me greatly.

'They're beautiful creatures,' I tell her, and she agrees.

I turn to find Suzette, but she's been drawn away to attend to important frog pageant matters. As I look around for her, one of the frog queens approaches me.

'Mr Connolly, can I have a selfie with you, please?'

It's Carly, from the Unmarried Division. How could I say no? And so we sit upon a wall and Carly prepares to take her shot.

'Do you need to be knowledgeable about frogs to be a frog queen?' I ask.

'Pretty much.' Carly pauses to inspect the picture. 'Actually,' she confides in me quietly, 'I'm scared to death of frogs.'

'Really?'

'I love the festival, but that's when I held one for the first time. And it was nothing like Kermit.'

I feel like a great weight has just left Carly's shoulders.

'I'm like that with spiders,' I tell her.

'I'm pretty much like that with anything that can't talk back but can crawl and jump on you,' she says. 'It gets that sissy part of your soul that touches you deep.'

We chat for a while longer, Carly and I, swapping stories about what beasties scare the bejesus out of us.

I've had a lovely time here in Rayne, which can truly consider itself to be unique in celebrating all things frog-related. What's more, by the time Suzette finds me again, it seems that time has been ticking. That a certain culinary item might've dropped off the frog tour of the city does nothing to weaken her smile, however, but everything to restore my appetite for later.

'We can still show you the frog murals around town,' she suggests, which suits me just fine.

Later, back on the train, I watch the last of Louisiana slip by my carriage window and feel a little sorry to be leaving. Everyone I've met has been so welcoming, and so proud of what is a strikingly diverse culture. From Chubby and his zydeco music to the Cajun backwoods, the food and the frogs, this Southern state strikes me as having far more to offer than meets the eye. There's the laid-back way of life down here that we're all familiar with, but behind it all the people are passionate about their culture and their environment, and we could all learn a great deal from that. As we head for New Orleans, the final destination for the *Sunset Limited*, I watch this wonderful patchwork of water and woodland slip by and hope that I'll be back again one day.

Later, having boarded the last train on my tour of America's outlying states, I have broken out my banjo once again. As the *Crescent* pulls out of The Big Easy, I begin to pick out a tune as we cross a wee bridge. I say a wee bridge, but actually I mean massive. Record-breakingly so. This is Lake Pontchartrain, and we're travelling across the longest water-spanning bridge in the world. It's nearly twenty-four miles long and a crazy experience because you feel like you're taking a train across the sea. Strictly speaking, Lake Pontchartrain isn't a lake at all. It's an estuary that feeds the Gulf of Mexico, and the banks are the inspiration for a classic Hank Williams song. Not that I sing that now.

The great man is on my mind as we head for our next destination and I hope you'll stay with me to find out why. But for now I have another song to get out of my system, and it begins like this: 'Oh, you cannae shove your granny off a bus …'

ALABAMA

This is the Heart of Dixie, also known as the Yellowhammer State after the local bird. We're crossing a plateau here, with lazy waterways making their way down to the coast. Aboard the *Crescent* we pass cane fields and farms with dilapidated trucks in the yard.

Life feels laid-back here, as it did in Louisiana, and that's just how I feel as the *Crescent* begins the steady climb from the south towards the north-east of the country. There are still plenty of places for me to look forward to visiting, but one in particular feels quite personal to me. I allow myself a little detour when we stop at Birmingham, and head 100 miles south to Montgomery, the Alabama state capital. I've got mixed emotions about this excursion. I'm excited but also a little blue, as most of us feel when visiting the grave of someone significant in our lives.

I'M SO LONELY: HANK WILLIAMS' GRAVE

When I was a little boy, aged about eleven or twelve, my father took me to a marketplace in Glasgow called the Barras. Its proper name is the Barrowland, but Glaswegians have shortened it in their own way. Now, this market sold everything, and in those days it sold records. That day, my father picked up a record by Slim Whitman called 'Dear Mary'. It was a big 78rpm single. He bought it because he thought it was a hymn to Mary, mother of Jesus. In fact, it was a love song to a woman called Mary, in which Slim sings about feeling weary without her. My father was disappointed when we got home, but I wasn't. I was delighted, because it was a very good song. So good that I learned to play it and even yodel in the right places.

When my father heard me he was flabbergasted, and also quite impressed. A few weeks later, one Sunday, we were back in the Barras. My father went up to the record guy and told him all about how I'd learned to play the tune. The guy explained it was a Country and Western song and sold him a record that changed my life. It's called 'Long Gone Lonesome Blues' by Hank Williams. He is my absolute hero to this day, with thirty-five Top Ten records in the USA and eleven Number Ones. And he was dead at twenty-nine.

Right now I am standing in a cemetery, here in the state capital of Alabama, in front of Hank Williams' grave. It's a towering but graceful affair, much like the man himself. That it's laid with AstroTurf to stop fans from taking the grass is a mark of superstardom, I think. It isn't holy ground, but that's how it feels, as I've thought about this moment so much. Respectfully, I step up to his headstone, inscribed with musical notes, carvings and the names of some of Hank's greatest hits. They're deeply personal and intense songs: 'I'm Still in Love with You', 'Your Cheatin' Heart' – my God, what a writer! Then there's 'Luke the Drifter', which was a persona Hank took on, always walking into the sun with a guitar over his shoulder. I was profoundly impressed, not just by the songs but by his look. In fact, Hank is responsible for my lifelong love of cowboy boots. I never went as far as the hat, but as you know, the reason why shall remain with me.

As I stand before his grave on a still, clear day, I remember that I emailed my daughter to say I was coming here. And she replied, quite simply, 'I'm so lonesome I could cry.' That's the effect he has on people. He died about the same time my father gave me that record, and now I find myself as close to the artist as I will ever be. So, with lip trembling, I want to say thank you, Hank. Although I can't say hello, I want you to know that I am still in love with you.

MAKING A STAND: THE BIRMINGHAM CHILD CRUSADERS

I've come to Birmingham, Alabama. This is a city that is slowly moving out of the shadow of its past. During the Fifties and Sixties, it was the most segregated city in the States. There were so many bomb attacks on black communities it became known as 'Bombingham'. In the midst of this struggle, an event took place designed to change hearts and minds. Across several days in early May of 1963, hundreds of black Christian children, some as young as six, gathered to march peacefully in protest against segregation. In response to what was dubbed the Children's Crusade, and as a measure of the times, perhaps, the police opened up water cannon, unleashed police dogs and arrested many of the young participants.

It's a shocking, shameful tale, indeed, and though it served to galvanise the Civil Rights movement and ultimately led to social change, the most striking fact of all is that the kids didn't fight back in the face of this oppression. They remained non-violent throughout, and so it's a great honour that four of those children have agreed to meet me. Only, they're not children any more, of course. They're wise old men and women, and shining examples of human beings at their finest.

I have so many questions to ask. It's so difficult to get my head around how any form of authority could turn on schoolchildren as they did.

'What persuaded you to march?' I ask, for this was no handful of kids out to make a noise on a whim. For days before the crusade, many pupils had mobilised themselves to put the word out and marshal support from their fellow students.

'The inequalities in our schools,' says Janice, a teenager at the time. 'I was born into a segregated society, but when the difference was brought to my attention I really wanted to do something about it.'

'Our equipment was so old.' Georgina is a serene woman with cropped hair and beautiful jewellery. As a pupil, she had been involved in the recruitment process ahead of the crusade. 'We had used books with pages missing, old typewriters and old furniture, but also we couldn't just pay our money to get on the bus, then take a seat. We had to put out our money, get off the bus, and go to the door at the rear.'

Even hearing this now, over forty years on, makes me uncomfortable.

'I can't imagine how that must feel,' I say. 'It must be so humiliating.'

Janice tells me about the dividing line.

'There was a little block of wood which said "Coloureds Only" on one side and "Whites Only" on the other side. So we couldn't sit in the whites-only side even if there were no seats on our side. We had to stand.'

'And if you were sitting down on a full bus and a white got on, the driver would shift the sign back and you'd have to move.' Alvin speaks quietly but with great authority, 'That's what happened to Rosa Parks. Only she refused to move.'

BJ sits across the table from Alvin, listening closely.

'They were denying us human rights,' she says, levelling her gaze at me, 'and we decided that we didn't want to live this way any more. Now, that upset them very bad because they wanted to continue to control us, keep us in bondage, keep us down and keep us under their foot.'

I am listening to powerful words here, and I simply nod in recognition. Janice explains how her mother and father's generation were intimidated into complying by the authorities.

'They had our parents over a barrel,' she tells me. 'If they'd gone out to demonstrate then they could have lost their jobs. But we weren't working, so we didn't really have anything to lose and everything to gain. They couldn't stop us,' she reasons. 'We weren't afraid. I really didn't know any white people. I didn't encounter white people in my neighbourhood, and certainly not in my church or school. I didn't know anybody to hate!'

I tell her that's one of the most impressive things about the nature of their crusade. But I want to know how their parents felt, knowing that their children were determined to take such a risk by standing up for their rights.

'Well, my mother did caution me before I left home,' says Janice. 'She told me: "I'm sending you to school, so don't you go and get yourself in any trouble!" I said: "Yes, Ma'am," and I did go to school. I just wasn't going to stay!'

With a glint in his eye, Alvin tells me that whereas he promised his mother that he'd go to school, he ended up going straight to jail. We laugh, but I cannot shake the fact that they were just kids at the time. Then Georgina shares her experience and I get an even stronger sense of just how determined they were to take a stand.

'My parents realised that I was going to go because I always felt like things were not right,' she says. 'Years later, when I was an adult, my mother said: "I just knew you would do it," but she never discouraged me from going.'

'But did you realise at the time you were part of something huge?' I ask, when we talk about how the marchers began to gather outside a local Baptist church.

Everyone shakes their heads.

'I never thought anybody cared,' said Janice. 'There had never been any indication when I was out marching. We came out onto the church steps at 16th Street and we sang "We Shall Overcome". Walking in pairs, we got maybe a block before police officers stopped us and told us that we were in violation of a city ordinance. They said we couldn't parade without a permit, and that we'd go to jail if we continued. Now, these were white men carrying guns, and that intimidated me, but then someone started singing "We Are Not Afraid", and that gave me the courage to remain in the line and go to jail.'

Georgina shares the story of her arrest, which occurred before she had even left the church.

'Out on the street, they had the police wagons backed up to the church. The doors were open, but they told us not to pull back inside the building as it would be considered as resisting arrest. We didn't want that on our records, so we ran *into* the wagons.'

'That must've surprised them,' I say.

'The police had dogs,' says Alvin. 'It was a frightening feeling.'

'Some folks got bitten and had to go to the hospital,' says Janice. 'People with their shirts torn and things. It was pretty traumatic.'

'I was downtown near the store,' says BJ. 'We heard all the fire engines. I thought there must be a fire somewhere. Then the truck showed up. The firemen jumped off with the hose and started spraying us. We were knocked down by the water, and they just *dragged* us to a little yellow school bus and took us to jail.'

'How did that feel?' I ask.

'Looking back,' says Janice, 'I was glad to be a part of it.'

'But it wasn't so nice to be behind those bars,' continues BJ. 'I was in there for three weeks, and treated really badly. They would tell us that Dr Martin Luther King was dead, or that our parents didn't want us any more. At five o'clock they would come by and rake a can across the metal doors to wake us up. Then they'd hand us each a toothbrush and a little pail of water. We would be ordered onto our knees in a straight line and made to scrub the jail floor.'

Georgina explains that so many child crusaders were jailed that the authorities ran out of space.

'That Monday when I was arrested, they had us in a fenced-in area outside the jail because it had reached full capacity. It was packed. Outside, it started storming and it rained so hard you couldn't see anything. So, they got us on a city bus and took us over to the state fairground. We didn't know where we were going. They just said: "Get up, you're leaving!"'

'That sounds terrifying,' I say.

'It sure was,' says Georgina. 'We were thinking that we were going to be lynched.'

'The interesting thing about going to the fairground was that normally blacks couldn't go there,' says Janice. 'I'd walked past it so many times, heard the music and smelled the popcorn and all those things. So, when those buses turned into the grounds we started cheering! Of course, they didn't let us ride anything. They carried us off to the facility there, but it was a lot better than being in the county jail.'

'That place was terrible,' says BJ. 'They would march us to an area and open up this big steel door. It was like a walk-in freezer, but they turned off the electricity so it wasn't cold. In fact, we called it the hot box. They would push us in, I mean hundreds upon hundreds of us. They were literally stuffing us in. Then they would close the door and leave us in there and we would scream and scream. You couldn't even see the person in front of you. It would get hot, and everybody was slithering and sweating. We couldn't breathe. People began to pass out and we would pound on the doors. They would yell: "Don't pound on these doors! Nobody can hear you anyway! Hush this noise or else we are going to beat you!" Finally, they took the big latch off the door and we just fell out. People were purple and blue and would have died if they had not opened those doors.'

A silence settles upon us for a moment.

'Do you think this was just to get power?' I ask.

'Well, they *had* the power,' says BJ in measured tones. 'They just wanted to teach us a lesson.'

I ask what happened after their jail ordeal. Did anyone end up in court?

'I did,' says Georgina, and unfolds a sheet of paper that she's holding: 'This is the summons they sent my parents. They said I was a delinquent and they were responsible for me, and so they had to appear in court for me.'

The document is a copy, she tells me, and I'm well aware that the original must be over five decades old. Even so, their memories of what happened have far from faded. Having listened to their experience, it could be no other way. What happened to the young crusaders like Georgina, Janice, Alvin and BJ provoked an outcry, not just locally but on a national level and all around the world. As a kid in Glasgow, I remember watching news reports about them. It was immense! Shortly afterwards, Birmingham's leaders agreed not just to release all the protesters but to implement desegregation across the city. The Civil Rights struggle didn't end there and the city would be struck that year by an appalling bomb attack on the church at 16th Street that killed four children.

Nonetheless, the child crusaders could claim a historic victory. Many years later, official pardons were issued to those involved. When I mention this, my friends around the table respond with mixed feelings.

'I didn't accept mine,' says Janice, who tells me she still considers her arrest to be a badge of courage.

'It was met with controversy,' BJ explains, who accepted her pardon. 'It was our decision to go ahead as a family and record this for history.'

Like Janice, Georgina turned down her pardon. 'But it never interfered with me getting a job,' she points out, addressing me with great poise in both her voice and her bearing. 'I was proud to put my arrest on my CV!'

As our conversation comes to a close, I tell them all how privileged and honoured I am to have met four people who changed the world for the better. As I leave, I'm also well aware that these exemplary individuals had no idea that they'd ever succeed at the time. What they went through is unimaginable, but that they came through it with such dignity and grace will remain with me for the rest of my life.

THE SCROLLWORKS ORCHESTRA: MUSIC FOR THE PEOPLE

Making my way across the streets of Birmingham, off to meet someone else who risked everything for the greater good, I remember the time I met Rosa Parks. It was a Hollywood showbiz event. It wasn't like I had earned an audience, but it still felt like I was shaking hands with history. Then I recall that the legendary producer and musician, Quincy Jones was present at the same party, and what an arse I'd made of myself in trying to be his best mate. At that kind of event, I used to just feel like this kid from Glasgow who had got lucky. I grew up listening to his music and always wondered what it would feel like to be so close to the guy that I could call him 'Q', like his inner circle. I'd met him a few times, was stuck with 'Quincy', but this time I just forgot myself. I called him 'Q' – and he didn't batter me! But then Sidney Poitier came up to him and said, 'Hey, *Cuesy*!' and I thought Shit, I'm not part of the in-crowd at all.

I smile to myself, and cringe a little at the memory, but it also distracts me from the fact that Birmingham is an awfully quiet place. Honestly, it's like a three-minute warning has gone off. I picture Yvonne back at missile command in Tucson, Arizona, preparing to twist her cheap little key. There's just nobody here. Not a soul on the street. It's dead. Sadly dead. I take solace in the fact that I'm heading for an oasis of hope and life in a city that evidently still struggles in many respects.

A few blocks down, I arrive outside St Paul United Methodist Church. This is the very heart of Birmingham's Civil Rights district and home to the Scrollworks Orchestra. It's dedicated to helping children of all backgrounds come together through music. It isn't an arts-funded project. To make it

happen, the woman responsible chose to give up her entire life savings. Normally, when I hear about someone who has done a saintly thing, my first response is to run a mile. But when I learned about Jeane Goforth, and the sacrifice she made for others, I just had to find out more.

Jeane is as humble as they come, as is often the way with living saints.

'I'm not really,' she says, with a note of embarrassment after I describe her in such lofty terms. 'But I am passionate about providing music to kids who wouldn't otherwise have a chance to play.'

Jeane is a softly spoken lady, bespectacled and with lovely rosy cheeks. She might not appear like a social activist, but first impressions count for nothing when you learn of her achievements. Now, when cuts are made to education budgets, music lessons are often the first to suffer. A true believer in the unifying force of music, Jeane couldn't stand by and watch as opportunities dwindled for young people in the area. Nor did she devote herself to raising funds to do something about it via raffles and coffee mornings. Instead, she withdrew all the money she had set aside for her retirement, headed for the inner city and started up a school of her own.

'How much did it cost?' I ask.

'Forty-five thousand dollars to start the programme,' she tells me, without even a hint of the personal sacrifice this involved. 'I decided I needed to go out and teach the kids that weren't getting music in their schools and didn't have access to an instrument. Music changed my daughters' lives, and I knew there were kids out there for whom it would be a passion, but they would never discover this for themselves if they didn't play. So that's what I wanted to offer them,' she finishes simply.

As any parent knows, offering kids a chance to pick up an instrument can be hard on the ears. The joy of Jeane's project lies in her recognition of the greater social harmony that can be had from bringing together disadvantaged kids with more privileged peers. Music is a great leveller, after all, and Jeane reminds me that it can also serve as a springboard for opportunity.

'A lot of the skills that they learn when they play music translate into skills they can use at school,' she tells me. 'It really helps in terms of cognitive development and self-discipline.'

We're talking in a basement room. From upstairs, as we speak, I can hear the strains of the orchestra limbering up. I'm busting to go see for myself.

As she leads me up a level, Jeane tells me that she was inspired by a revolutionary programme in Venezuela that aimed to turn kids from the poorest neighbourhoods into music stars.

'And do you get results here?' I ask.

'Oh, yeah,' she says. 'This year, we got five kids accepted at the Alabama School of Fine Arts, which is huge. Most of the kids that come here get accepted into college, and do really well.'

The contrast between Jeane's quiet voice and the achievements she describes is striking. Then she pushes through a door into the main part of the church. Before us, the orchestra strikes up for a performance of Beethoven's 'Ode to Joy'. Settling into a pew alongside her, I take a moment to register the diversity of both the children and their instruments. The musicians are accompanied by a small choir, and held together by an energetic conductor. The result is plaintive, accomplished in some places and scratchy in others, but deeply moving. There's just so much to read between the musical lines here. Listening to these kids, drawn from all walks of life, I begin to understand what persuaded Jeane to stand up and make Scrollworks a reality. It gives me a glow just thinking about it, and I wonder how rewarding it must feel for this woman who gave up so much to make it happen.

Without a doubt, I feel I am in the company of a very special lady, and the kids are just fantastic. The odd flat note is what makes it feel so real. These boys and girls aren't all natural-born talents, but their enthusiasm is boundless, and they clearly take such pride in being a part of something special. You know, it's lovely how a guy from the Gorbals can take his music to Hong Kong, for example, and it's instantly recognised by his Chinese counterpart. And they can both go to Tibet and play there, and their music is immediately understood and appreciated for what it is. Music is just a great communicator. And you can't communicate with someone on that level and stay enemies. Even if some seemingly wise individual tells you to be wary of a certain race or religion, when you're playing together you cannot stay enemies. Without Scrollworks to bring these kids together as one orchestra, I can only imagine how they might've regarded each other. But watching them now is a joy.

I focus on a boy playing the drums. He looks bored shitless, I think at first. Then I realise that in fact he's just trying to be cool. Jeane leans across and tells me that the wee lad who plays the trombone is desperate to play the tuba. I've never met anyone who is desperate to play the tuba before. Jeane says he's been promised that if he sticks with the trombone for a year then he'll be moved up to the tuba. That's brilliant, you know? So lovely. I hope he sees his dream come true.

What sticks with me more than anything, however, are the parting words of the conductor. For these kids had come in especially to perform for my visit and be filmed by the crew.

'I really appreciate you guys showing up today and volunteering to be here,' she tells them. 'I know it's out of our usual schedule, so big kudos to you and your parents. It means a lot that you are here, and it's a really good showcase for Scrollworks.' The children are packing up their instruments as she addresses them, but they all listen closely. 'In twenty years,' she continues, 'you will look back and show it to people and go: "Look at me when I was little and cute!"'

Her comment provokes much laughter, but she's right in a greater sense. Being on telly is neither here nor there, but this opportunity to come together across social divides is surely a gift that will serve them well throughout their lives.

AND ON A BUM NOTE ... VULCAN'S STATUE

Before I leave Birmingham, I feel it's my duty to lurch from the sublime to the ridiculous. For I've heard about a local landmark that has my name written all over it.

In 1903 the good people of the city commissioned the sculptor Giuseppe Moretti to build a monumental statue. They wanted it to represent the power of the area, the mineral resources and the work ethic. In response, Moretti chose to build an image of Vulcan the Roman god of fire and forge. At fifty-six feet tall, upon a towering podium overlooking the city from parkland, it is officially the largest cast-iron statue in the world.

But what makes Birmingham's Vulcan so remarkable is not so much the scale. As soon as I lay eyes on him, a muscular, spear-wielding giant, I realise I will never forget this moment. It's a powerful and impressive piece of work, but there's no hiding the fact that the guy's arse is hanging out of his toga. This is no god, I think to myself. He's an arse-onist. That's what he is. OK, I'm outta here …

As well as inspiring endless bad jokes, the sight of Vulcan's bare buttocks upsets many people. I'm not entirely sure why, for it's a perfectly nice bum. Honestly, we're talking about a pair of sculpted cheeks that I'd be perfectly happy to carry around myself. I suspect the negativity is down to the fact that the offending backside faces the direction of an upscale housing quarter. While the statue continues to divide local opinion, it's also served as a beacon for road safety awareness. For forty years, Vulcan's spear was replaced with a neon torch. On days when there had been a fatal traffic accident in the city, the torch would switch from glowing green to red. I can't help wondering how many accidents occurred as a result of the driver being distracted by an enormous butt crack on the skyline.

All in all, it's probably one of those sights best appreciated from a train.

MARYLAND

Having crossed states so vast they're bigger than some countries, it's a joy to arrive in one so snug I might've missed it altogether had I nodded off for a few minutes. Instead, knowing that I'm set to make a stop here, I make the most of the rolling scenery. We pass forests and woodland groves as well as small well-to-do towns, and it all looks very cosy to me.

It's also a little bit deceptive, because Maryland boasts six million residents, which makes it one of the most densely populated states in America. The capital, Washington DC, is close by, and so it's no surprise that this outlying region is so attractive. At the same time, I'm well aware that we're closing in on another landmark city – sadly, this one has a reputation for mean streets and hard times.

Baltimore is a seaport, built on industries that are now in decline or dead, and has an air of grit about it. This isn't just a first impression by a long-distance rail traveller. It's a dangerous place, with more murders in the last year than New York – despite being far smaller. We're in the home of the hard-boiled crime series, *The Wire*. Many areas are run through with racial tension and social deprivation, and I hope that one day soon fortunes will turn for this historic city. There's still a great deal to enjoy here, though, from the Railroad Museum to the crab shacks in the bustling harbour area. But above all, there's one particular thing that I've come to see on my stopover here and it involves a trip to the morgue … never say that I don't take you anywhere nice!

THE MURDER DOLLS: *CSI* IN MINIATURE

Frances Glessner Lee was born into Chicago high society in 1878. She had her heart set on a medical career, but her father wouldn't let her pursue it. She got married, had children and life rolled on. But then the marriage failed. Divorced and in her fifties but with a sizeable inheritance to call upon, Frances decided that it wasn't too late to turn an interest in forensic pathology into a career. To do so, she donated a large sum of money to Harvard Medical School in order to establish a department dedicated to the subject – the first of its kind in the USA. There, she combined her studies with another passion – for miniature model work – and set about building cutaway dolls' houses.

No, Frances hadn't lost the plot. She began to create tiny crime scenes, based on true cases, for use in the department's seminars. Mysterious or unexplained deaths formed the subject of eighteen dioramas in total, each culled from court cases or visits she made in person to the grisly scenes. Each of these dioramas, at an exact 1:12 scale, was designed for student medical examiners to ponder at their leisure while figuring out exactly what had happened. Most notable of all is the fact that Frances put these cutaways together with such remarkable accuracy and attention to detail that they formed the foundation for many aspects of modern-day crime scene investigation.

Her collection of dioramas, *The Nut Shell Studies of Unexplained Death*, takes its name from a saying amongst detectives. You can just picture those old gumshoes muttering, 'Convict the guilty, clear the innocent, and the truth will be uncovered in a nutshell.' I love that, and looking at Frances's tiny snapshots of violent and brutal crimes, I am fascinated by her work. Her objective was quite simple: to encourage forensic students to study a scene of crime in close detail and thereby reduce the risk of overlooking or contaminating clues. It's said that this sharp-eyed matronly lady formed the basis for the central character, played by Angela Lansbury, in the television series *Murder She Wrote*. There's certainly no doubt that Lee's work serves as an inspiration not just to aspiring medical examiners but to anyone with an appreciation of creative detail.

'Each one was built by authentic construction methods.' My guide, Bruce Goldfarb, is Assistant to the Maryland Chief Medical Examiner. Bruce is smartly dressed and authoritative. He looks like he might've uncovered evidence to put away a villain or two in his time. We're in a display room inside the Medical Examiner's Office, standing over a wee diorama of a child's nursery. The tiny walls are decorated in floral pink, along with an upward spray of blood above the cradle. There, a doll baby with mottled skin and a traumatic head wound lies dead.

It's the recreation of a murder scene in miniature, and the detail really is the most striking thing about it.

'Behind the walls is a real home frame,' Bruce points out. 'It took as long to build as a real house and each one cost what a house cost to build.'

I look up with a start. Frances Glessner Lee enjoyed the luxury of being a millionaire heiress, but I am still flabbergasted at the costs involved. Then again, each house is made with incredible attention to every last millimetre. Windows really open, keys turn in locks. Letters on tables have been faithfully recreated to the final full stop. Almost everything I see has been made from scratch, Bruce tells me. In a way, it's a celebration of accuracy. I ask my guide if it's true that Frances once recreated a scale rocking chair that when pushed would rock exactly the same number of times as the original. Bruce smiles, as if that's one of his favourite anecdotes about her.

'She insisted everything had to be totally accurate and everything had to work. She was fanatical about detail. All the wood came from a barn on her property. She employed a carpenter and her son, who would saw off just a sixteenth of a centimetre from the surface and use it as timber. There was no cutting corners with her, and all the fabric, the materials, the furniture, the blood spatters, the detail work … that's all by her own hand.'

'And where did she learn these skills?' I ask.

'Her background talent was in fabric needlework,' says Bruce. 'In a sort of subversive way, Frances used her womanly skills to break into this old boys' club. She was a real trailblazer.'

I move from one scene to the next, in awe at the undertaking.

'Seeing that everything is in miniature,' I say, 'aren't the clues in miniature, too?'

Bruce tells me they are indeed teeny and by extension harder to find.

'It could've been done to size,' he says, 'but that would've been impractical. Frances just thought it would be terrific if she could bring a crime scene to the classes at Harvard. It's all about observation,' he continues, explaining that each gory diorama contains a secret to explain the death. 'Seeing what you can see with your eyes; what clues, what direct and indirect evidence you can gather. At a homicide seminar there might be four or five police officers assigned to one model. They spend hours just looking at it, and finally they present their conclusions to the rest of the group. You can tease out an amazing amount of information from each model.'

'I guess it means you have to look very closely.'

As we inspect each scene in turn, peering in with a penlight that makes it look all the more sinister, I'm aware that we're looking at recreations of poverty. There are no Cluedo-style mansion houses here, and yet each one has been assembled almost lovingly. It's as if Frances genuinely cared for these characters.

'A lot of these people are alcoholics or prostitutes,' Bruce tells me. 'These aren't people she would've interacted with, and yet she would've spent a lot of time at these crime scenes and her work provides a glimpse into their lives.' As he speaks, I peer in at a little bathroom. A lady is sprawled dead in the tub. Her limbs have been arranged exactly as she would've been found. It's undeniably sad to think this is based on a real-life scenario, but equally fascinating to see it at this scale. Bruce is quick to point out something so minor I would've missed it. 'Frances noticed that there would have been a worn spot in front of the toilet,' he says. 'There are even mineral deposits in the bath-tub. I don't know how she managed that, but there they are.'

I have to squint to see this for myself, and Bruce is quite right.

'That's extraordinary,' I say.

'Her work is really popular with doll-house enthusiasts,' he tells me, which comes as no surprise. 'They go crazy over these things. The detail is just phenomenal. It is truly mind-blowing,' he stresses, which must mean something, coming from a man who has curated the collection for years.

'Is that a bottle of booze on the counter?' I ask.

'I believe it is.'

All of a sudden, my inner detective is itching to get out.

'Is she supposed to have got drunk and fallen in?'

I turn to Bruce, hoping he'll declare the case closed. His face gives nothing away.

'That is a possible scenario,' he offers, much to my frustration. 'The answer and the solutions are kept secret, so I can't actually tell you.'

In a bid to break his resolve, I move on to the next scene. At first glance, it looks like nothing untoward has happened. I'm looking at a bedroom scene, and I have a sneaking suspicion that the man under the blanket might be stone-cold dead.

'What happened here?' I ask, effectively giving up.

Bruce picks out details with the penlight: a radiator and a bucket of beer bottles. I am none the wiser.

'Well, this fellow worked at an ice cream factory,' he reveals, which is a lead. At least, Bruce presents it as such. I just look at him blankly. 'He's been using dry ice in that bucket to chill his beer. And the next morning he's dead.' Next, I try to read Bruce's mind, but that doesn't get me far. Had the victim died from an ice cream overdose? Bruce keeps the penlight trained on the radiator. 'I just love how behind the radiator there's a panel to get moisture in the air,' he says, momentarily distracted by such exquisite detail. 'Anyway, the next thing that happens, the guy wakes up dead.'

'So, I'm looking for clues here.'

I scan the scene and I know that Bruce is watching me closely.

'Do you know what dry ice is made out of?' he asks finally.

'No.'

'Carbon dioxide.'

'Ohhhhhh!' I say, as the penny drops.

Now, I may not be a master chemist, but I'm pretty sure that as a bucket of dry ice turns to gas in a confined space it would make breathing a wee bit challenging.

Bruce shrugs, unwilling to confirm my realisation that this man most likely suffocated in his sleep.

'I'm just putting it out there,' he says.

Now I'm getting into the swing. I want to try another one. We step across to a domestic scene of shocking violence. Even though I'm looking at a doll, I can't ignore the fact that it's based on a real event.

Now what's happened here? I ask myself. I'm looking at a kitchen and a bloodied body sprawled upon the tiles.

'This is Dorothy,' says Bruce. 'She was found in a house next to a church. She was terribly brutalised. She has all kinds of wounds – bite marks, strangulation, etc.'

'She's still got a knife sticking out of her,' I observe, but it's hardly a Sherlock moment. The handle is the first thing I spotted.

'This is a sad one,' Bruce continues. 'Dorothy went to the butcher's store. Her mother had sent her to get some ground beef.' He points out the package of meat on the counter. 'Anything about it strike you in particular?'

I notice a hammer lying on the tiles. Bruce remarks that it's bloodstained and asks if I think she came home in a hurry.

Based on the evidence, I have no idea whatsoever.

'What do you think?' I ask instead.

'Well,' says Bruce, 'you'll note that there's no sign of bleeding from the knife wound.'

'Which means she was stabbed *after* death!'

At this point, I begin to kid myself that the world of police procedurals lost out when I chose stand-up comedy as a career.

'Dorothy wasn't reported missing for four or five days,' Bruce tells me, 'and yet the meat—'

'Hasn't gone off?' I suggest with all the confidence of a small boy who has just learned to ride a bike.

Bruce tries hard not to look disappointed.

'Well, the meat is pretty rotten if you look closely. But the body isn't. And that is all part of the puzzle.'

I begin to realise that I might need a couple of hours, or even a week, to come close to cracking this case, and so we move on. Over the course of the next hour, I'm introduced to one crime scene after another. Before I can get into whodunnit, however, I can't help but keep marvelling over how it was all made. I spot a wee mini ashtray, complete with mini cigarette butts.

'They have tobacco in them,' Bruce confirms. 'She rolled them, burned them, and then stubbed them out to create an ashtray full of cigarettes.'

Looking at the bigger picture, I find my gaze lingering on each one as if a clue might slowly materialise.

Then, together, we dwell on the case of a woman found slumped against her bathroom door by the building's janitor. Naturally, I assume the janitor did it, because we all know they're always guilty. Once again, I am proven wrong. With prompting from Bruce, I see that I am in fact looking at the scene of a suicide, in which the poor woman hanged herself before the noose snapped.

'That's what it looks like,' Bruce agrees, and then toys with me. 'Or was it staged to look that way?'

Bruce plays his cards close to his chest for a reason. These are teaching aids, after all, designed to encourage you to make your own deductions. The suicide scene sits alongside another one featuring an apparent hanging from a loft joist, but Bruce is more interested in highlighting that every one of the papers strewn underneath the victim has been handwritten, just as Frances had found them.

'How on earth could she do that?' I ask.

Bruce sweeps the light across the loft, as if to pick out clues.

'With a pin,' he tells me, and then leaves me to my own devices.

The next scene features a moving part. Bruce encourages me to pull on a cord. It lifts the pillow from a bed, where another dead body lies.

'Is that lipstick?' I ask when I see the red mark on the underside of the pillow. 'So she was suffocated!' I add, as the penny drops again.

Bruce withdraws the beam from the penlight, returning the scene to the shadows.

'So, you got one down,' he says, finally.

'Constable Slow to the rescue,' I reply.

As we continue our investigation into these little lives, I do come to appreciate that taking your time is key here; working through clues and sifting through evidence in search of that elusive truth. I find the process fascinating, and each scene a treat to behold. So I'm quite shocked when Bruce tells me that soon after Frances passed away in the early Sixties, a question mark hung over the future of her collection. Her death brought an end to her funding contribution to the forensic department and so Harvard mothballed the project.

'These model crime scenes were thirty years old by then,' says Bruce. 'I guess it takes time to appreciate their true value.'

Fortunately, the Medical Examiner's Office recognised both the artistry and the potential practical use for the houses. The project was moved here to Baltimore in the mid-Sixties, restored in the Nineties thanks to a fifty-thousand-dollar grant, and continues to be in active use as a forensic learning tool for homicide detectives. The centre even has a life-sized 'nutshell room', I learn, funded by the international best-selling crime writer, Patricia Cornwell.

'We can do everything in there,' Bruce tells me. 'Hangings, suicides, stabbings, carbon monoxide poisonings. We also have lots of props: weapons, victims, fake drugs – although every time I look inside there are less and less fake drugs,' he adds, and flattens his lips together for a second. 'Someone has been smoking pencil shavings.'

'Are the nutshell seminars popular?' I ask.

'Sold out,' Bruce tells me, and I'm delighted to hear it. 'This year is the seventieth anniversary of the first one. In about a month from now we'll have another room full of police officers, and they will be doing the same thing that we're doing now.'

'That's wonderful,' I say, peering into another scene of domestic hell. 'To be doing this in a high-tech age.'

'This is timeless,' Bruce agrees. 'But sadly, the facts of timeless death do not change. Murder is murder. You can strangle, shoot or stab, but there are only so many things that you can do. Some things are internal, and violent death is one of them.'

It's a poignant end to an engrossing tour. I've had such fun on the trail of the truth, despite my limited success, but Bruce reminds me that Frances assembled these masterful creations for a deadly serious reason.

'I'm glad they exist,' I say, on thanking my guide for such an enlightening experience.

'You couldn't do this with photography,' says Bruce. 'You couldn't do this with film. I don't even think you could do this today with virtual reality. You need a three-dimensional model you can examine at your own leisure from whatever angle you want. You just can't do that with any other medium, even in this day and age.'

ANDY'S DINER: FOOD FOR THE SOUL

Before I leave Baltimore and clamber back on board the *Crescent* for the last short stretch to New York, I decide to seek out something to eat. Now, in all the years that I've been touring America, I always finish with the same food. A hot dog. It's usually from an airport and isn't much good, much like the one I had at the high school football match in San Antonio. Things will be different this time, however. If you ask anyone in Baltimore for a hot dog recommendation they'll point you in the same direction. The place has such a solid reputation that I imagine even the guys off the street will tell you to visit the same place. So, here I am, outside the G&A Diner.

This is an all-American restaurant and not some artificial affair put together to please the tourists. It isn't just the solid stainless steel counter and row of stools from which customers suck milkshakes through straws or sip oil-black coffee. Nor is it the photos-through-the-ages on the walls or the ranks of booth tables, most of which are occupied. It is in fact the welcoming presence of the owner, Andy Farantos, that tells me this is the real deal. The guy extends his hand to greet me and offers a firm handshake. He has salt-and-pepper hair, slicked back neatly, and a cloth slung over his shoulder. If I could choose to stand here in any decade since the 1950s, I sense that Andy would look no different.

'I hear your hot dogs are extremely good,' I say.

'The best, sir. The best.' Andy's accent wouldn't sound out of place at a casting for a Martin Scorsese movie. 'But we gotta big menu,' he points out. 'Cheese steaks, cheeseburgers, fish and chips if you want it. I can put it on newspaper with malt vinegar?'

'Actually, I had my heart set on a hot dog,' I confess.

This is clearly not a problem for my attentive host.

'Whatever you got your heart set on, you're gonna have,' he says.

Without further word, Andy sets to work. I watch with nothing but admiration as he lines up four, five and then six sliced hot dog buns from the palm of his hand to the crook of his elbow, ready to be filled.

'I love your arm technique.'

'There's a lot of business around here,' he tells me, 'and when they come in here it's a lot easier just to knock them out this way. The place seats a hundred and twenty people, so you know you've gotta get it done. I have a great crew, half of them are family, the other half isn't, but we're all family, you know? Lot of people have been working here a long, long time. I've got plaques on the walls of ladies who worked here for thirty-four years. This place, it made a lot of people … not wealthy,' he offers, and then finds the word he's looking for – 'It made them happy.'

Quick as a whippet, Andy goes on to dress each bun with a hot dog, chilli sauce, diced onion and mustard. This time, I find my mouth watering at the offering presented to me. And it tastes as good as it looks. I imagine customers have been standing in this spot for years, savouring something done so simply and to such perfection.

'How long has this place been here?' I ask, relishing every mouthful.

'Since 1927,' says Andy. 'My grandfather and his cousin started it, and my dad bought it off him with my Uncle Jimmy in 1966. Then I bought it off them in 1988. And the key word is "bought" it,' he stresses. 'When something is given to you, you tend to let it go a little bit, you know? I've seen a lot of places get handed to somebody and they just let it slide.'

'Where did your grandfather come from?' I ask.

'Greece,' he tells me, and there is pride in his eyes. 'He came over with my cousin, settled in Coney Island for a while, but even when they moved down here and opened this place they could barely speak any English. Their names were Gregory and Andy. So, they called it the G&A Coney Island Restaurant.'

'As simple as that,' I say.

'Yessir.'

'That's great.' I wipe my mouth with a serviette. 'It's an American story, isn't it?'

'It's literally the American dream. Our whole family came over from Greece. Eventually my uncles started coming over. They all worked here and then they migrated to Williamsburg in Virginia back in the Fifties and Sixties. That's when they started buying pancake houses, lobster houses, steakhouses. They all did very well, courtesy of this place. It's housed a lot of people that have gone on to do big things.'

As he shares his story, Andy doesn't stop working for even a moment. He prepares more hot dogs, serves coffees and clears plates, and does so at lighting speed. The family didn't just strike lucky, I think to myself. They worked hard to build a future for themselves here in the USA, which to my mind sums up the immigrant spirit.

'What kind of customers do you have?' I ask.

'The best,' he says, 'and from both ends of the spectrum. You name it, from homeless guys that scrounge up some change for a soup to the owner of the Baltimore Orioles baseball team.' Andy tells me that when his grandfather and cousin first went into business, they stood out by refusing to have a 'Whites Only' sign hanging in the doorway. 'Everybody was welcome,' he continues. 'They were from the old country, and they didn't care who's who, what's what, black or white, didn't matter to them. You know, they got a lot of flack for it but in the end everybody came back.'

'Wonderful,' I say, and I could apply the same word to the hot dog.

'This is a big blue-collar area, from back when we were the number one steel producer in the USA. And when I say blue-collar, I mean guys who feed their families, take care of their families, do everything right.'

I'm mindful of Baltimore's struggling economy as he tells me this.

'That kind of industry is disappearing isn't it?'

Andy acknowledges me with a weary sigh.

'General Motors shut down three years ago and Bethlehem Steel has gone. It was heartbreaking, as a matter of fact. One time I was coming over the bridge and they were demolishing the plants. We're talking about big, big furnaces to melt the steel, and it was all—' Andy pauses there, as if consulting his memory. 'You know, we watched it come down, and you're watching a place that employed anywhere between five thousand and thirty-five thousand people, depending on the time of year and the era. So that's hard times. I'm not doing the math right now in my head but I can tell you, sixty to seventy thousand jobs are not available in Baltimore now 'cos those big plants have closed.'

'I'm amazed you're still here at all,' I say, thinking of the impact this must've had on the wider community.

'Yeah, well, we've been through our thing,' he admits, but the fact that I'm here talking to Andy now is testament to the fact that people will always turn to good honest food to lift their spirits. A smile crosses his face just then and he invites me to look down the length of the counter. 'You see the fades,' he says, and points out dull patches along the surface. 'That's where it's been worn down from people's elbows, just sitting there eating their hot dog and everything.'

'Oh, that's great!'

Andy spreads his hands.

'Like I said, it's all a dream,' he says, then looks around. 'The way this room was made is the way it is. It's probably just a little bit narrower because of all the layers of paint, but it's also my silver screen,' he adds playfully. 'I've seen the whole world go by in here, and the changes, too. You know, everybody's OK, everybody's happy. Then the economy dips and everybody dips. But I tell you, even when people don't have money, they're just happy here. Some of the best people I've ever met, right here in this neighbourhood, great people.'

I scrunch up my serviette and lay it on my empty plate.

'That is the best hot dog I've ever eaten,' I say, and I speak with the same sincerity that Andy has just extended to me.

14

THE END OF THE LINE

I board the *Crescent* for the last time, with mixed emotions. It's only a short journey to New York's Penn Station. A couple of hours at the most. That's nothing when I reflect on the time I've spent looking out of train windows, travelling through America's outermost states.

This trip has been a joy, and above all else an education. I have laid eyes on a landscape that shifts from rugged mountains to verdant valleys and bone-dry desert, cradling communities and industries both old and new. It's been an adventure into the past, a snapshot of the present and a taste of the future in many ways.

Later, when Manhattan's all-familiar skyline begins to take shape, I spot new structures going up that I haven't seen before. In a strange way, this comes as a comfort. For all the social, industrial and economic challenges the country faces – and this experience has brought many home to me – America continues

to look ahead with great confidence, as it has always done. This is down to the rich tapestry of her people, I feel sure, and although I have met just a handful since leaving Chicago, each and every one of them has left a lasting impression on me. From the dope farmer to the cattle rancher, the frog princess (Unmarried Division), the residents of Tent City, the Williston oil workers and even the elderly mall walkers back in Minnesota, they all have hopes and dreams – wherever they may find themselves in life – and believe that this is the country that will enable them to achieve them. Even the elephant seals must beach themselves on the West Coast for a reason.

As the train pulls into the platform at Penn Station and the sliding doors open for the final time, I wish everyone I've met along the way peace, love, good humour and prosperity. I also want to thank you all for joining me. You've been splendid company and I've enjoyed every moment. Stepping off with my banjo over my shoulder, I'm struck by a thought that brings a smile to my face. For in a way this is how it feels to be a modern-day hobo. Deep down, I realise, there's one inside us all. Heading across the concourse, slowly melting into the crowd, I make my way towards the exit and the sunshine outside with my head held high. For this might be the end of one fascinating journey, but as ever it marks the beginning of another – and that will never end.

Stepping off with my banjo over my shoulder, I'm struck by a thought that brings a smile to my face. For in a way this is how it feels to be a modern-day hobo. Deep down, I realise, there's one inside us all.

THE TEAM

SEATTLE

WASHINGTON

PORTLAND

SHELBY

GLASGOW

WILLISTON

MONTANA

NORTH DAKOTA

SAN LUIS OBISPO

CALIFORNIA

LOS ANGELES

ARIZONA

TUSCON

EL PASO

TEXAS

SAN ANTON